CONTENTS

Look for these boxes

Biographies

These boxes tell you about the life of inventors, the dates when they lived, and their important discoveries.

Setbacks

Here we tell you about the experiments that didn't work, the failures, and the accidents.

EUREKA!

These boxes tell you about important events and discoveries, and what inspired them.

Any words appearing in the text in bold, **like this**, are explained in the glossary.

TIMELINE

2010 – The timeline shows you when important discoveries and inventions were made.

BEFORE SUBMARINES

Submarines are special boats that travel underwater. Before submarines were invented, people did not know much about the world deep below the ocean's surface. They dived in shallow water to explore and to find things such as shells and treasure.

People need to breathe in **oxygen** from air to stay alive. Divers held their breath or carried sacks full of air underwater. The air did not last long, which meant divers needed to return to the surface often to breathe in more air. People could stay underwater longer when they carried on breathing in air from the surface through hollow reeds, which were like straws. These were the first **snorkels**.

Divers with snorkels can only breathe underwater when they are close to the surface.

around 3000 BC – Greek divers use hollow straws to breathe while underwater

THE
SUBMARINE

Richard and Louise Spilsbury

www.raintreepublishers.co.uk

Visit our website to find out
more information about
Raintree books.

To order:

☎ Phone 0845 6044371
📄 Fax +44 (0) 1865 312263
✉ Email myorders@raintreepublishers.co.uk

Customers from outside the UK please telephone +44 1865 312262

Raintree is an imprint of Capstone Global Library
Limited, a company incorporated in England and Wales
having its registered office at 7 Pilgrim Street, London,
EC4V 6LB - Registered company number: 6695582

Text © Capstone Global Library Limited 2011
First published in hardback in 2011
Published in paperback in 2012
The moral rights of the proprietor have been asserted.

Edited by Louise Galpine and Laura Knowles
Designed by Philippa Jenkins
Original illustrations © Capstone Global Library Ltd 2011
Illustrated by KJA-artists.com
Picture research by Mica Brancic
Originated by Capstone Global Library Ltd
Printed and bound in China by CTPS

ISBN 978 0 431118 44 4 (hardback)
15 14 13 12 11
10 9 8 7 6 5 4 3 2 1

ISBN 978 0 431118 51 2 (paperback)
16 15 14 13 12
10 9 8 7 6 5 4 3 2 1

British Library Cataloguing in Publication Data
Spilsbury, Louise.
The submarine. -- (Tales of invention)
623.8'205'09-dc22
A full catalogue record for this book is available from
the British Library.

Acknowledgements
We would like to thank the following for permission to
reproduce photographs: Alamy pp. **6** (© LondonPhotos
- Homer Sykes), **17** (© Tara Carlin); Corbis pp. **19**
(© Bettmann), **23** (© Bettmann); Getty Images pp. **5**
(MPI/Hulton Archive), **11** (MPI/Hulton Archive), **12**
(De Agostini), **13** (Stock Montage/Hulton Archive),
15 (Hulton Archive), **21** (National Geographic/Emory
Kristof), **22** (National Geographic/Emory Kristof),
26 (Photo by BAE Systems), **27**; iStockphoto p. **4**
(© Christophe Schmid); © Mary Evans Picture Library
2007 p. **8**; NavSource Naval History p. **18** (US Navy
photo courtesy of Darryl Baker. Negative scanned
courtesy of By Design, Benicia, CA); NOAA p. **25**
(Institute for Exploration/University of Rhode Island);
Photolibrary pp. **10** (North Wind Picture Archives), **20**
(Brand X Pictures); Rex Features p. **7** (Roger-Viollet),
www.navy.mil p. **14** (US Navy, Chief of Naval Operations
Submarine Warfare Division (N87)).

Cover photograph of John P. Holland standing in the
conning tower of his submarine, *Holland VI*, April
1898, Perth Amboy, New Jersey, USA, reproduced with
permission of Corbis/© Bettmann.

We would like to thank Ian Graham for his invaluable help
in the preparation of this book.

Every effort has been made to contact copyright holders
of material reproduced in this book. Any omissions will be
rectified in subsequent printings if notice is given to the
publisher.

Diving bells

Diving bells were heavy containers made of metal, wood, or glass that people used to go underwater. An object floats in water when the upwards push on it from the water (called **upthrust**) is greater than the downwards force of the object's weight. Diving bells sank because the downwards force of their weight was greater than the upthrust. The bell trapped a big bubble of air so people inside it could breathe.

Here a diving bell helps people to find items from a shipwreck in 1752.

EUREKA!

The Greek king Alexander the Great used a glass diving bell in 332 BC. There is a legend that he saw a sea monster that was so big it took days to swim past the bell!

332 BC – Alexander the Great uses a diving bell

1578 – William Bourne publishes a book called *Inventions or Devices*. It contains his ideas for how to make a working submarine.

THE FIRST SUBMARINES

It took the efforts of many different inventors over hundreds of years to develop the submarines we know today. One of the earliest problems inventors solved was making a submarine **watertight**. If water filled the submarine, the people inside it might drown.

The *Drebbel*

Cornelis Drebbel invented the first submarine in 1620. People thought it looked like two wooden rowing boats, one stuck on top of the other. It had a short tower on top, with a door for people to get in and out. People inside rowed the machine along using oars through the sides. The whole machine was covered with greased leather to stop water getting in any gaps, but it was probably still rather damp inside.

This is a model of the *Drebbel*. It was similar in shape to some modern submarines, but it would have been far less comfortable inside.

EUREKA!

Drebbel continued to improve his inventions. His third submarine was his biggest. Thousands of people stood on the banks of the River Thames in London when Drebbel's amazing submarine took its first public voyage in 1623. The submarine slowly carried along 16 passengers a few metres below the river's surface. It stayed underwater for about three hours.

1620 – The *Drebbel* is the first successful submarine

Cornelis Drebbel (1572–1633)

Cornelis Drebbel was a Dutch inventor who worked for King James I of England. He used ideas of the British inventor William Bourne to help invent his successful submarine. As well as his submarine, Drebbel invented many other things, including a microscope and a machine that told the time, date, and season.

 1634 – A French priest and scientist called Marin Mersenne writes that submarines should be made of copper and shaped like long cylinders to move easily through the water

Ups and downs

Drebbel is said to have put heavy weights inside his submarine to make it sink. Making an object heavier in relation to its size or **volume** increases its **density**. There is more **upthrust** on a hollow metal boat than on a solid ball of metal of the same weight because its density is lower. Drebbel could only make his submarine rise by getting rid of the weights to lower its density.

EUREKA!

In 1680, Italian inventor Giovanni Borelli invented **ballast tanks** so his submarine could rise and fall. He wrote about filling goatskin bags inside the submarine with water from outside to increase the submarine's density and make it sink. Then the water would be squeezed out of the bags to lower the submarine's density and make it rise.

This drawing from 1683 shows the ballast tanks inside Borelli's submarine.

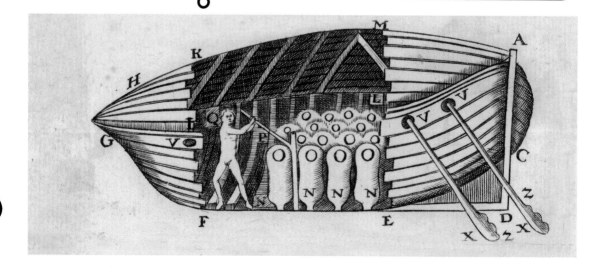

1653 – The *Rotterdam Boat* is invented but never works

The carpenter's submarine

The English carpenter Nathaniel Symons invented a submarine with a changing volume in 1729. He sat inside and turned a handle to pull the two halves of the submarine together or spread them apart. When the halves were spread apart, the submarine rose up in the water because it had a bigger volume, and so it was less dense. When the halves were pushed together again, the submarine sank because it had a smaller volume and a greater density.

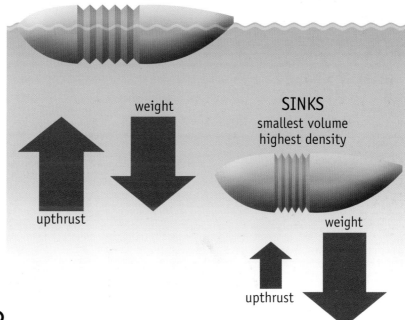

FLOATS
biggest volume
lowest density

weight

upthrust

SINKS
smallest volume
highest density

weight

upthrust

The red arrows in this diagram show how a submarine's volume affects how much upthrust is pushing on it and whether the submarine sinks or rises in the water, even though its weight stays the same.

9

Sneaking up on the enemy

As submarines improved, governments of different countries realized they could use them to sneak up and attack their enemies. In 1653, the French inventor De Son made the *Rotterdam Boat* for the Belgian navy. They planned to use it to ram holes in British navy ships. Unfortunately, it was too heavy to be moved by the sailors inside it!

The *Rotterdam Boat* was the first submarine designed to attack enemy warships, such as these.

1680 – Giovanni Borelli invents the ballast tank to change the weight and **density** of a submarine

1680   1690   1700

The *Turtle*

The *Turtle* was the first submarine to attack an enemy warship. This wooden, egg-shaped machine was invented by the American David Bushnell in 1776, during the American Revolution. The *Turtle* could move underwater towards enemy British ships, drill holes in their bottoms, and attach clockwork **mines** to blow them up.

It was very cramped inside the *Turtle* submarine. There were handles and foot pedals to spin the **propellers**, move the **rudder** outside, and to fill or empty the **ballast tanks**. Because it was such hard work to operate everything at once, the *Turtle* could only move very slowly.

The *Turtle* got its name because its curved shape looked like a turtle's shell. This 1776 illustration shows what it looked like inside.

Setbacks

On 6 September 1776, Sergeant Lee, an American, moved the *Turtle* next to a British ship called the *Eagle* in New York harbour. He tried to drill a hole in the ship but failed to attach the mine. Lee ran out of air and had to come to the surface, where the enemy chased him off.

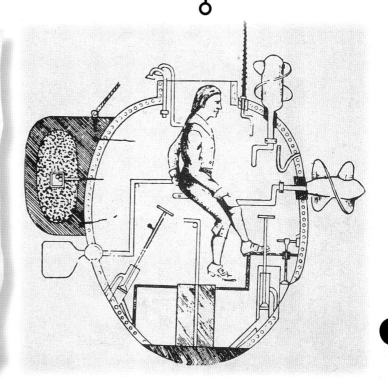

IMPROVING SUBMARINES

When a submarine moves through water, **drag** slows it down. Drag is the push of water you can feel when you swim in a pool. A submarine can move faster if it has a smooth, **streamlined** shape because water flows more easily past it, reducing the amount of drag.

The *Nautilus*

In 1797, Robert Fulton designed a new submarine with a streamlined, metal body that would allow it to attack enemies faster. The *Nautilus* had a sail so that it could use wind to move on the water's surface. The sail folded down once the *Nautilus* dived so it did not increase drag underwater. To move underwater, a handle was turned on the inside to work a **propeller** outside.

The *Nautilus* was designed to move more quickly through water than earlier submarines.

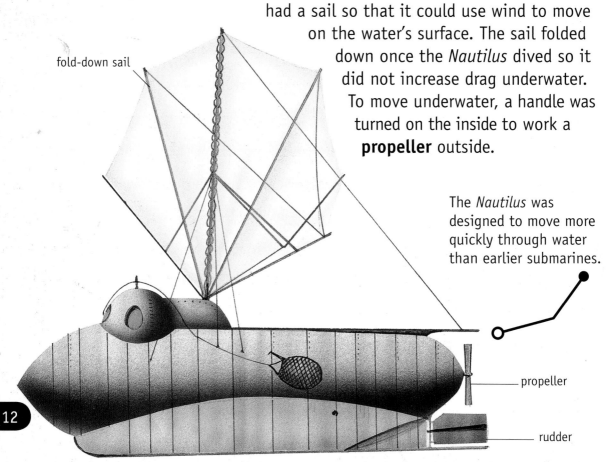

fold-down sail

propeller

rudder

1729 – Nathaniel Symons builds a submarine that can change its **volume**

Robert Fulton (*1765–1815*)

American artist Robert Fulton was only a teenager when he made
paddle wheels to move a fishing boat on water. Soon he became
fascinated by the idea of a "plunging boat". In 1800, Fulton paid to
have the *Nautilus* built. He hoped the French government would
buy it to use in their war against Britain. The French first thought
fighting with submarines was cowardly, but they were impressed
with Fulton's submarine in trials. When the *Nautilus* was used in a
real attack, it was too slow to catch a British ship. Fulton broke his
submarine up and moved on to inventing steamships instead.

Breathing problems

When we breathe in air to get **oxygen**, we breathe out **carbon dioxide**. This gas is poisonous if you breathe too much in. The first submarines could not stay underwater for long because carbon dioxide built up inside them. They could only stay underwater for a long time if the submarine stayed near the surface so the crew could take in fresh air through **snorkels**.

In 1861, Brutus de Villeroi invented the USS *Alligator*. This was the first submarine with a system for keeping the air fresh. Pumping air through a bottle of special liquid removed the carbon dioxide.

The USS *Alligator* was 4 metres (47 feet) long. Like today's submarines, it had a **streamlined** shape and an air-cleaning system.

1776 – David Bushnell invents and demonstrates his *Turtle* submarine

Weapon of war

During the American Civil War (1861–1865), one side offered money to
submarine inventors who could sink enemy navy ships. The *H.L. Hunley*
submarine, named after the man who paid for it, sank the USS *Housatonic*
in 1864 by ramming an explosive harpoon into its side. After this success
the *H.L. Hunley* also sank, but nobody knows why.

This illustration shows the inside
of the *H.L. Hunley*. The crew of
eight turned the **propeller** fast
enough to ram enemy ships.

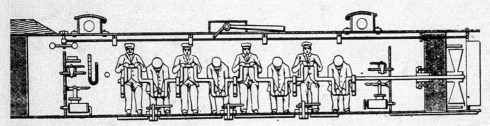

1797 – Robert Fulton
invents the *Nautilus*

SUBMARINES WITH ENGINES

Objects move forwards through water when the **thrust** (the force moving them forwards) is stronger than the **drag**. Early submarines were slow because sailors could not turn the **propellers** fast enough to create a strong thrust. This changed when people invented engines to create more thrust. Today, powerful engines turn giant propellers to thrust submarines fast through the water.

Air power

The *Diver*, invented in 1863 by Charles Burn and Simon Bourgeois, was the first submarine with an engine. The engine used **compressed air**, which is air forced into a small space, for power. Air moved fast from air tanks into a tube-shaped cylinder. This pushed on a piston (a type of plunger) inside. When the piston moved, it turned a **crankshaft** connected to a propeller. The engine had several cylinders with pistons that together spun the propeller fast.

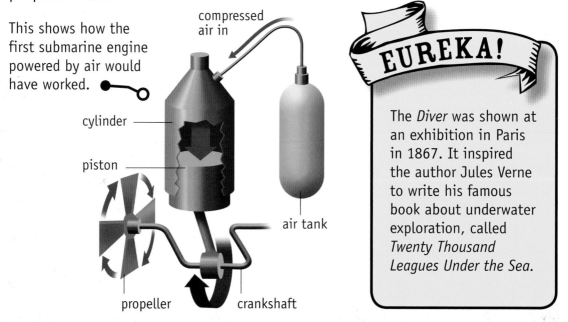

This shows how the first submarine engine powered by air would have worked.

compressed air in

cylinder

piston

air tank

propeller   crankshaft

EUREKA!

The *Diver* was shown at an exhibition in Paris in 1867. It inspired the author Jules Verne to write his famous book about underwater exploration, called *Twenty Thousand Leagues Under the Sea*.

The first torpedoes

In 1866, Robert Whitehead invented **torpedoes**.
These are underwater weapons that allow submarines
to attack enemies safely from a distance. The first
torpedoes were long tubes packed with explosives.
They had compressed air inside that thrust them
forwards when it was released. Today, torpedoes
have engines inside them and they can steer
themselves towards their targets.

This illustration shows
a modern submarine
launching a torpedo.

Electric submarine

In a **steam engine**, coal is burned to heat water. The hot water produces steam that moves pistons and turns wheels or **propellers**. People found that it was not good to use steam engines inside submarines because burning coal used up the **oxygen** that sailors needed to breathe, and made lots of heat and smoke.

In 1897, John Philip Holland invented the *Holland VI* submarine, which used **battery** power. A battery is a store of electricity. Electricity from the batteries made an electric motor turn the propeller. The *Holland VI* also had an engine that burned petrol to power the propeller. Sailors ran this engine when the submarine was near the surface to move the submarine and to recharge its batteries.

This *Holland VI* submarine belonged to the US Navy.

John Philip Holland (*1840–1914*)

John Philip Holland was an Irish schoolteacher who spent half his life inventing submarines. His sixth submarine, the *Holland VI*, was the most successful. It held six sailors and could travel 50 kilometres (30 miles) underwater before the batteries needed to be recharged. The submarine could stay underwater for 40 hours but it was very cramped onboard. Holland sold many bigger and faster versions of the *Holland VI* to the British, Japanese, Russian, and United States navies. One of Holland's last inventions was a machine designed to help sailors escape from damaged submarines.

19

1863 – The *Diver* is the first submarine with an engine, powered by **compressed air**

1864 – The Spanish submarine *Ictineo II* is the first submarine to use steam power at the surface and a different chemical engine underwater

1864 – The *H.L. Hunley* is successfully used in the American Civil War

1866 – Robert Whitehead invents the **torpedo**

1870

1880

Nuclear submarines

During World War I (1914–1918) and World War II (1939–1945) all submarines used electric motors. In 1954, the United States Navy launched the first nuclear submarine. The *Nautilus* had a **steam engine**, but the heat to make the steam came from a **nuclear reactor**. This is a sealed container filled with special metals that keep releasing heat for years.

Nuclear submarines could go faster and further than electric ones. They did not need to come to the surface to recharge **batteries** or return to land to get more fuel. The trouble with nuclear reactors is that they are very expensive and dangerous if they go wrong. Today, most big navy submarines are nuclear, but many smaller submarines are still electric.

Here, a nuclear submarine surfaces through Arctic sea ice.

EUREKA!

In 1958, the *Nautilus* became the first submarine to travel under the thick sea ice of the North Pole, from the Atlantic to the Pacific Oceans. The submarine stayed underwater without surfacing for a distance of about 3,000 kilometres (1,800 miles).

1897 – John Holland builds the petrol and electric *Holland VI*

Submarine comforts

Modern nuclear submarines can weigh more than 24,000 tonnes (23,500 tons) – as much as 200 blue whales – and can carry 150 sailors. They are much more comfortable for sailors to live in than earlier submarines. They have bedrooms, showers and toilets, and a restaurant open 24 hours a day. They have special machines to turn seawater into drinking water and to keep the air fresh.

These crewmen are relaxing in the cramped spaces of the nuclear submarine NR-1.

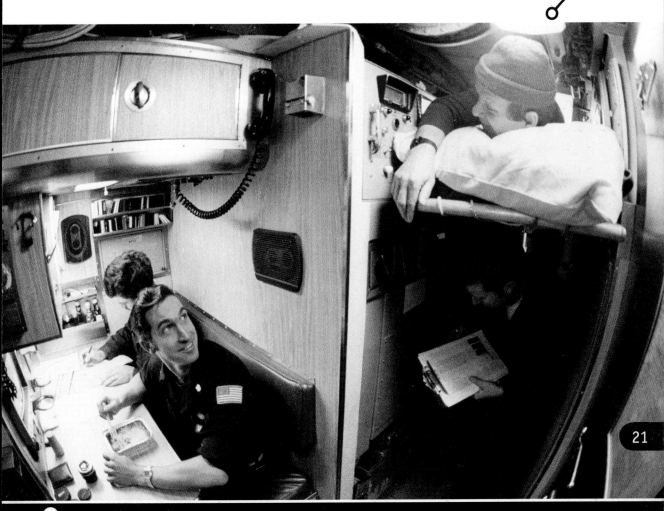

1902 – Simon Lake invents the modern submarine **periscope**

1910

1920

EXPLORING THE OCEANS

The deeper a submarine goes underwater, the more water there is above it. The weight of this water pressing down is called **water pressure**. To go really deep underwater, inventors had to make submarines to survive the enormous water pressure there.

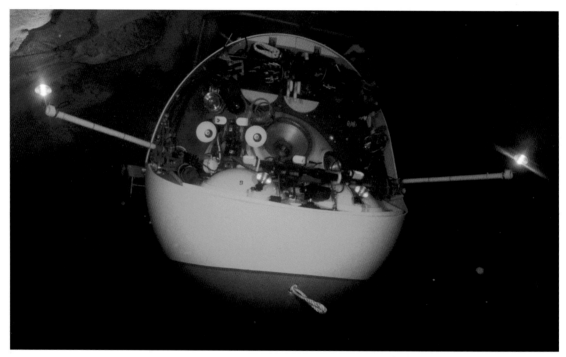

Water pressure at a few tens of metres deep could force in water through gaps in the **hulls** of early submarines. Their hulls could collapse and windows could crack. Many of today's submarines have hulls made of very strong steel that is more than 15 centimetres (6 inches) thick, and windows made of even thicker glass or plastic. Now submarines can dive hundreds of metres deep into the ocean.

Here, the Mir2 is about to reach the Mid-Atlantic Ridge, on the bottom of the Atlantic Ocean.

1940

The deepest submarine

Only seven submarines with people inside have ever dived deeper than 3 kilometres (1.8 miles). In 1960 the *Trieste*, invented by Auguste Piccard, went down to almost 11 kilometres (7 miles) deep. The people inside sat in a small metal sphere that was part of the hull. This shape is best at coping with high water pressure, which at that depth was like having 50 jumbo jets sitting on top of the submarine!

Here, the *Trieste* is being lowered into the sea.

EUREKA!

In January 1960, Jacques Piccard and Donald Walsh reached the bottom of the Marianas Trench near the Phillippines in the *Trieste*. The trench is the deepest point of all the oceans.

23

1948 – Hyman Rickover develops a small **nuclear reactor** that is designed to power a submarine

1953 – Dimitri Rebikoff invents the first **ROV** submarine

1954 – USS *Nautilus* is the first nuclear submarine

1950

1960

Looking above

From inside a submarine, sailors can look above the water for enemy ships by using a **periscope**. Periscopes are long tubes with angled mirrors inside. Light from the outside hits the top mirror, reflects down through the periscope, and off the lower mirror.

Early periscopes were not very good. In 1902, American inventor Simon Lake created a better version with **lenses** inside. Lenses are discs of glass that help to enlarge and focus what sailors can see through a periscope. The periscopes on today's nuclear submarines have digital cameras that can show the view on a computer screen.

This diagram shows how a periscope is used for looking above the surface of the water.

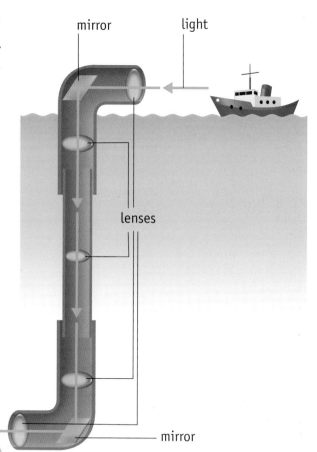

mirror

light

lenses

mirror

1960 – The *Trieste* carries out the deepest manned dive in history

1964 – The magnetic sea engine is invented

1981 – The first Typhoon class nuclear submarine, the biggest ever submarine, is launched by the Russian Navy

1960

1970

1980

Submarines without people

In 1953, an inventor called Dimitri Rebikoff made the first robot submarine. It was called POODLE and did not need people on board to control it. Rebikoff operated his machine by sending computer instructions along a cable from a ship on the surface. Machines such as this are called Remote Operated Vehicles (**ROVs**). ROVs are usually small so they can explore shipwrecks and other places that larger submarines cannot.

EUREKA!

In 1986, Robert Ballard used the ROV *Jason Jr.* to take the first photographs inside the world's most famous shipwreck, the *Titanic*. This ship sank to the bottom of the Atlantic Ocean after crashing into an iceberg in 1912.

Here, ROV *Jason Jr.* can be seen exploring the *Titanic* shipwreck.

1986 – ROV *Jason Jr.* takes the first photographs inside the *Titanic* shipwreck

INTO THE FUTURE

Submarines have changed a lot since they were first invented 400 years ago. Today submarines are bigger, more **streamlined**, and faster. They can dive deeper, travel further, and stay underwater longer. In what ways could submarines change in the future?

Some modern submarines are massive. Here, the newly built HMS *Astute* submarine is being transported to the sea.

No propellers

In the future, submarines may move around without **propellers**. Some may pump jets of water backwards to make themselves **thrust** forwards. Others may use special **magnets** to make a jet of water thrust them forwards. In 2007, James Tangorra invented a robot fish fin that could make an **ROV** thrust forwards, change direction, and also hover on the spot. It uses less electricity than propellers.

2004 – Rob Innes builds the *Seabreacher* submarine

2008 – The *Super Falcon* submarine is launched

Underwater tourism

The *Super Falcon* submarine, invented by Graham Hawkes in 2008, is built for two people. It is shaped like a small fighter aircraft. It is light, fast, and has long wings that help it to dive. On some coasts, such as those in Hawaii in the United States, there are already large submarines that take tourists on trips underwater. In future, tourists may stay at underwater hotels and explore the oceans in their own personal submarines like the *Super Falcon*.

The *Seabreacher* personal submarine can roll and even leap out of the water.

EUREKA!

Keen surfer Thomas Rowe designed a robot dolphin submarine after watching dolphins playing in the waves. His student Rob Innes later built the *Seabreacher* submarine based on Rowe's designs.

TIMELINE

3000 BC
Greek divers use hollow straws to breathe while underwater

332 BC
Alexander the Great uses a diving bell

1578
William Bourne publishes a book called *Inventions and Devices*. It contains his ideas for how to make a working submarine.

1862
The USS *Alligator* is the longest, most advanced submarine in the world

1852
Lodner Phillips invents a submarine **propeller** that can angle to steer the machine

1797
Robert Fulton invents the *Nautilus*

1863
The *Diver* is the first submarine with an engine, powered by **compressed air**

1864
The Spanish submarine *Ictineo II* is the first steam-powered submarine

1864
The *H.L. Hunley* is successfully used in the American Civil War

1866
Robert Whitehead invents the **torpedo**

2008
The *Super Falcon* submarine is launched

2004
Rob Innes builds the *Seabreacher* submarine

1986
ROV *Jason Jr.* takes the first photographs inside the *Titanic* shipwreck

1981
The first Typhoon class nuclear submarine, the biggest ever submarine, is launched by the Russian Navy

1620
The *Drebbel* is the world's first successful submarine

1634
A French priest and scientist called Marin Mersenne writes that submarines should be made of copper and shaped like long cylinders to move easily through the water

1653
The *Rotterdam Boat* is invented but never works

1776
David Bushnell invents and demonstrates his *Turtle* submarine. It is the first submarine able to move independently above and below the water

1729
Nathaniel Symons builds a submarine that can change its **volume**

1680
Giovanni Borelli invents the **ballast tank** to change the weight and **density** of a submarine

1897
John Philip Holland builds the petrol and electric *Holland VI*

1902
Simon Lake invents the modern submarine **periscope**

1948
Hyman Rickover develops a small **nuclear reactor** to power a submarine

1964
The magnetic sea engine is invented

1960
The *Trieste* carries out the deepest manned dive in history

1954
USS *Nautilus* is the first nuclear submarine

1953
Dimitri Rebikoff invents the first **ROV** submarine

GLOSSARY

ballast tank compartment in a submarine that can fill with water or empty to make it sink or float

battery device storing chemicals that produce electricity

carbon dioxide gas in air that living things breathe out, or that is produced by burning fuels

compressed air air reduced in volume and increased in pressure. Bicycle tyres stay firm because they are filled with compressed air.

crankshaft shaft that turns when engine pistons move up and down

density how heavy something is for its size, or volume

drag force acting against the movement of a person, animal, or vehicle

hull frame or body of a submarine or boat

lens glass or plastic object that makes an image clearer or bigger

magnet piece of metal that attracts metal objects towards it

mine type of hidden bomb. Most mines explode when something touches them.

nuclear reactor machine to control the release of energy from special metals

oxygen gas in air that living things need to breathe in

periscope device shaped like a tube that allows someone to see over the top of something else

propeller device with two or more blades that pushes through water when it spins

ROV short for Remote Operated underwater Vehicle; robot submarine without people on board that is operated from a distance

rudder device to control the direction a submarine or ship moves in

snorkel tube to breathe in air from the surface while underwater, or a tube on a submarine letting air in and exhaust gases out from a working engine

steam engine engine that produces steam to move parts, usually by burning fuel such as coal

streamlined having a smooth, even shape to move easily and quickly through water

thrust force pushing a vehicle. A submarine has an engine and propeller to create thrust through water

torpedo long, narrow bomb fired underwater, usually from a submarine

upthrust upward pushing force acting on an object in water

volume amount of space that something takes up

water pressure push caused by the weight of water

watertight not letting any water leak in

FIND OUT MORE

Books

Bushnell's Submarine: The Best Kept Secret of the American Revolution, Arthur S. Lefkowitz (Scholastic, 2006)

Great Inventions: Submarines, Rebecca Stefoff (Marshall Cavendish, 2006)

How It Works: Ships and Submarines, Steve Parker (Miles Kelly Publishing, 2009)

Machines Close-up: Modern Warships and Submarines, Daniel Gilpin (Wayland, 2009)

Websites

Take a virtual tour of a submarine at:
www.njnm.com/LingInteractive/ling.html

Find out more about life on a submarine at:
americanhistory.si.edu/Subs/operating/aboard/index.html

Discover more about the *Seabreacher* personal submarine at:
www.seabreacher.com

Places to visit

Royal Navy Submarine Museum
Gosport, Hampshire PO12 2AS
www.rnsubmus.co.uk

The U-Boat Story exhibit
Birkenhead, Merseyside CH41 6DU
www.u-boatstory.co.uk

INDEX

acknowledgements

Heartfelt appreciation goes to all our friends, colleagues and students who supported and encouraged us in the development of this manuscript. A big thank you to Hodder Arnold for making it possible for us to write this book – especially Tamsin Smith and Katharina Hyland – also Nicola Jenkins who inspired the idea for this series and encouraged us to be part of it. Thanks to tutors/therapists Linda Ayers and Caroline Bray who reviewed our proposal, made helpful suggestions, and contributed interesting stories. Thanks are also due to our students and colleagues who contributed case studies – Carolyn Abdoolah, Vandana Mendonca, Gavin Blundell, Kim Hayden, Janna Land and Gina Darcy. Particular thanks to Narendra Mehta who works tirelessly to promote the art of Indian Head Massage across the globe and is a source of inspiration to us and many others. Special appreciation to our families for their unwavering support, particularly Terry Barnes for his help with the proofreading and Patrick Doyle for doing the housework!

The authors and publishers would like to thank the following for the use of photographs in this volume:

p.3 (left) © MAPS.com/CORBIS; p.3 (right) © Tim Graham/Alamy; p.4 (left) © Phillipe Lissac/Godong/Corbis; p.5 © The Print Collector /Alamy; p.6 Wellcome Trust Photographic Library; p.7 © Ausloeser/zefa/Corbis; p.8 Narendra Mehta; p.11 G Brad Lewis/The Image Bank/Getty Images; p.13 http://www.healer.ch/; p.17 © ArkReligion.com/Alamy; p.27 Science Photo Library; p.28 Dr P. Marazzi/Science Photo Library; p.38 Cheryl Power/Science Photo Library; p.39 (left) © Indigo/Alamy; p.39 (right) Bildagentur-Online/th_foto/Science Photo Library; p.40 (left) Dinodia Photo/Photolibrary.com; p.40 (right) Paul Poplis/Photolibrary.com; p.42 (left) Christi Carter/Photolibrary.com; p.42 (top right) John Glover/Photolibrary.com; p.42 (bottom) © Will & Deni McIntyre/CORBIS; p.43 (left) © iStockphoto.com/Moritz von Hacht; p.43 (right) © Francois Gohier/ardea.com; p.44 © J.Garcia/Photocuisine/Corbis; p.52 (top) © Medical-on-Line/Alamy; p.52 (bottom left) The Wellcome Trust Photographic Library; p.52 (bottom right) © Medical-on-Line/Alamy; p.53 © By Ian Miles-Flashpoint Pictures/Alamy; p.77 © iStockphoto.com/Sharon Dominick; p.80 (left) Cordelia Molloy/Science Photo Library; p.92 © iStockphoto.com/Susan Stewart; p.108 (left) Cordelia Molloy/Science Photo Library; p.108 (right) Busse Yankushev/photolibrary.com

Commissioned photographs © by Carl Drury.
With thanks to our model Anthea.

contents

When I learned that two of my students intended to write a book about Indian Head Massage, I was inspired by Mary and Lesley's vision. I felt proud to think that the popularity of this therapy merited another book.

Now that I have had the opportunity to read *Indian Head Massage in Essence*, I believe that Mary and Lesley can feel truly proud of their unique contribution to the world of holistic therapy. This book really reflects what I knew already: that Mary and Lesley's dedication to treating and training others would shine through every page.

I am certain this book will be of immense benefit to seasoned practitioners and to everyone who is curious about Indian Head Massage. It is full of useful information.

I especially liked the sections on marmas, self-care and the history of Ayurveda and its connection with Indian Head Massage.

When you read what Mary and Lesley have written, I feel sure you will gain insights which will lead to your personal growth and deeper interest in Indian Head Massage – a therapy which is close to my heart.

In fact, I'm pleased to witness the growth of Indian Head Massage both in the United Kingdom and around the world. My wife Kundan and I have been honoured with many invitations to teach Indian Champissage. We have trained in the USA, Canada, Australia, Japan, Hong Kong, Turkey, Germany, Spain, Sweden, Finland and Eire.

The popularity of Indian Champissage is spreading!

Many articles have been written, many students have been trained and many heads have been massaged. All this has added to the global popularity of this therapy. I truly believe that Indian Head Massage is a wonderful way to relieve most of the stress-related symptoms of the twenty-first century.

With the publication of this book, I hope that everyone who opens it will feel as excited as I do when you read what Mary and Lesley have written about Indian Head Massage from their uniquely personal and professional perspective.

Their words cast fresh light on this age-old therapy and the truly beautiful illustrations illuminate their well-researched and thoughtful text.

It is with the greatest of pleasure that I commend this book to students and lovers of Indian Head Massage the world over.

Narendra Mehta
Director, The London Centre of Indian Champissage International

introduction

Indian Head Massage is one of the most popular complementary therapies available today. Like many complementary therapies, it focuses on holistic care, concentrating on maintaining and improving health rather than just treating pain and disease. The term 'holistic' comes from the Greek word 'holos' meaning whole or complete. The holistic approach takes into account the physical, mental, emotional and social factors in a person's life rather than just a diagnosed disease or condition. Holistic practitioners consider the effects of integral biology when consulting with a client before treatment. Integral biology is the study of our environment's effects on our physical and mental health, because everything we do in our daily lives can have a positive or negative effect upon our bodies. For example, a cramped living environment can cause stress and related conditions such as anxiety and depression. Lack of exercise and a poor diet may cause similar problems, while a balanced diet and regular exercise can promote positive energy, vitality and mood. Many of the advancements of our modern world, such as computers, mobile phones, processed food, chemicals and pollution, can have damaging effects on our minds and bodies. Holistic care aims to create balance and harmony in the body, a state known as 'homeostasis'.

Indian Head Massage is probably the most accessible holistic treatment available as it requires no undressing or use of specialist equipment and can be done almost anywhere. It can benefit all age groups, from calming down over-excited children and anxious teenagers to providing nurturing touch for the elderly. It is particularly suited to the busy office environment as it quickly relieves stress and can even be done in the office chair!

The techniques are easy to learn and target areas of the body most vulnerable to the effects of stress and tension. Whether you are new to massage or an experienced therapist wishing to add this wonderful skill to your repertoire, as you learn the techniques of Indian Head Massage, you will find yourself much in demand among your friends, families and clients. You will also learn some self-help techniques to enable you to deal with your own everyday stresses and strains.

Although the name may suggest that it only works on the head, the treatment also works on the shoulders, arms, neck and face, releasing the tension that builds up in these areas due to poor posture as well as emotional and physical stress. It stimulates the circulation of blood and

1

lymph, encouraging efficient delivery of oxygen and nutrients to the hair and scalp, and aids the elimination of waste products. Following a treatment, clients often report feeling deeply relaxed or newly invigorated. The many other benefits of Indian Head Massage are described in this book and you will learn how techniques can be adapted to suit the situation or the individual client. We hope that you will enjoy learning this fascinating new skill and that it will enhance your life (and your practice if you are a therapist) as much as it has done for us.

history

About India

Mark Twain, the American writer and traveller, went to India in 1896 and wrote:

> 'Nothing has been left undone either by man or nature to make India the most extraordinary country that the sun visits on its rounds.'

India is a unique country; many see it as mysterious while to some it is the most magical land on earth. It is a land of contrasts with its bustling cities, dusty plains, lush forests, dramatic mountains, meandering rivers and vast coastline. It is scattered with sacred sites marking its rich history, and its landscape, sounds, aromas and people have inspired many epic stories and films. India has endured hundreds of years of foreign invasion and influence, yet its unique character remains untouched.

For centuries, India's spiritual and healing traditions have inspired and influenced people across the globe. Famous for its rich religious

India, land of many contrasts

Mother Teresa

traditions, four of the major world religions (Hinduism, Buddhism, Jainism and Sikhism) all have their origins in India. Travellers with a quest for adventure and self-discovery are drawn to its saints and sages, its yogis and gurus ('gu' means darkness, 'ru' means light). Local people and travellers contemplate life together in its ashrams (retreats). India has the power to touch the heart and soul like no other country. It was the adopted homeland of Mother Teresa (1910–1997), Nobel Peace Prize winner, world famous for her compassion and work with the poor; and the birthplace of many current day spiritual aspirants.

Today, many countries across the globe embrace India's influence – its religious traditions, yoga, cuisine, and system of Ayurvedic healthcare. In recent years Indian Head Massage has also become hugely popular and benefited many.

The Vedas

To trace the history of Indian Head Massage, we first look to the ancient Indian texts. The Vedas, the oldest scriptures of Hinduism, were composed between 1500 and 1200 BC. 'Veda' (meaning 'knowledge') is from the ancient Sanskrit language, a classical language reserved for religious and scholarly use. These scriptures were originally formed of four main books, which included topics such as health, astrology, poetry and ethical living. Legend says they were composed from direct communication with the Divine received during meditation. These sacred texts form the basis of Ayurveda from which Indian Head Massage evolved.

Ayurveda

The word 'ayur-veda' is Sanskrit and means 'life knowledge', the science and wisdom of life. In traditional Ayurveda there was no distinction between physician and priest and good health was seen as an integral part of spiritual life. This ancient healing system is based on the principle that health is not just about the absence of disease. It is a holistic healthcare system that aims to balance mind, body and spirit and encourage the body's natural healing abilities. Ayurveda recommends the use of diet, herbs, cleansing, yoga, meditation, massage, and chakra balancing as important practices of a holistic lifestyle because when life is lived well, longevity usually follows.

Ayurvedic texts describe the science of massage using marma points – vulnerable or sensitive zones on the body, used for diagnosis and treatment of disease as well as promoting health and longevity. These are similar to points used in Chinese acupuncture but extend to larger areas of the body and include vital organs like the heart as well as bones and joints.

The Vedas were inspired by Divine communication received during meditation

People from many countries visited India's Ayurvedic schools to study its medicine and it is thought that knowledge of Ayurveda spread out from India to influence the ancient Chinese medical system and other forms of medicine. For this reason, Ayurveda is often referred to as the 'Mother of all Healing'. In the sixteenth century, Paracelsus, known as the father of modern Western medicine, developed a system of medicine that was greatly influenced by Ayurveda. Ayurvedic texts were translated into Arabic and were frequently quoted by Avicenna, one of the most outstanding Arab physicians (980–1037).

Ayurveda went through a period of decline in India when Western medicine became dominant during the era of British rule. It became a second-class option, used mainly by traditional spiritual practitioners and the poor. After India gained its independence in 1947, Ayurveda regained its popularity. Today there are more than five hundred Ayurvedic companies and hospitals and several hundred schools of Ayurvedic medicine. Although it still remains a secondary system of healthcare in India, the trend toward complementary healthcare is increasing and Western and Ayurvedic physicians often work side by side.

Interest in Ayurveda in the West began in the mid 1970s as teachers from India began visiting the United States and Europe. By sharing their knowledge they have inspired a vast movement toward body–mind–spirit medicine. Today Ayurvedic colleges are opening throughout Europe, Australia, and the United States and Ayurveda has again become a respected and widely used system of healing in India and around the globe.

Massage

It is generally thought the word massage is derived from the Arabic 'mass' or 'mash', meaning to press softly. In Greek it means 'to knead', and in Sanskrit it is called 'masch'. Massage has been recorded in various forms for over 5000 years, with the earliest records from China dating back to 3000 BC. Archaeologists in Egypt discovered tomb paintings showing images of people being massaged. The famous Greek physician Hippocrates (460–377 BC), who is regarded as the 'Father of Medicine', described massage as 'the art of rubbing'. He recommended that massage using oils should be taken daily after a perfumed bath. Today, we instinctively rub or hold a painful muscle to bring about relief just as early man did.

Massage was used extensively by great kings and rulers to treat bodily ailments. Julius Caesar (100–44 BC) had daily massage to treat trigeminal neuralgia, an intense pain in the facial nerve.

Dr. Ambrose Paré (1517–1590), a physician to four French kings, used massage in his practice and is reported to have restored the

Julius Caesar received massage to treat neuralgia

5

health of Mary Queen of Scots by the use of massage alone!

Modern massage

Modern massage is generally attributed to Swedish fencing master and gymnastics teacher Per Henrik Ling (1776–1839), who developed a system of movement he found helpful for improving his health and physical condition known as the 'Ling system'. After a trip to China, where he was impressed by their massage skills, he combined his knowledge of gymnastics and the human body with Chinese philosophy to form the 'Swedish Movement System'. However, there is some debate about the origins of Swedish massage. Evidence indicates that it was in fact a Dutch physician, Johan Georg Mezger (1838–1909) who was influenced by Ling and systemised massage as the 'Swedish Massage' we know today. As French was the language of science and medicine in Europe at that time, French names were given to the basic massage strokes. Swedish massage may be defined as 'the manipulation of soft tissue for therapeutic

purposes'. It was traditionally performed with talcum powder applied over the body with deep pressure. Most therapists now use oils for their beneficial effects on the skin.

Massage was used during the First World War to treat patients suffering from injury and shell shock. Some hospitals established a massage department to treat patients. One of these was St. Thomas' Hospital in London, which had a massage department until 1934. After the Second World War, mechanical methods of treatment began to replace manual methods and this led to a decline in the use of massage and a lack of awareness of its benefits.

Massage declined in popularity in Europe during the late nineteenth and early twentieth centuries and was even regarded as a dubious practice due to its use in brothels. However, it has once again become a reputable and recognised therapy, thanks to increased awareness of the benefits of more natural and holistic types of treatment. Many different kinds of massage exist, but most are based on Swedish massage principles. Massage benefits all body systems and is useful in treating many types of physical and psychological problems.

Massage in Indian life

Massage features in many parts of life in India and traditions and skills have been handed down through the ages. It is customary for brides and bridegrooms to be massaged with special oils to promote health, relaxation, beauty and fertility. Expectant mothers are massaged to help them cope with childbirth, and mothers and babies receive a daily massage for around 40 days after the birth.

Massage is considered important in bonding and communication as well as promoting good health. In India, babies usually receive a daily massage until they are three years old and are then taught to share massage with family members on a regular basis.

Georg Mezger 1838–1909

Head massage

In Ayurvedic marma therapy, the head is the most important area of the body and massaging this area can benefit the whole person. By stimulating the supply of blood to the head, thoughts become clearer. The supply of blood to the pituitary and pineal glands increases – our growth, health and vitality depend on the proper functioning of these two glands. The lightest touch is registered by the brain and gently touching the crown of the head calms and soothes with immediate beneficial effects on the nervous system.

The yogis were ancient practitioners of Ayurveda and they considered the head to be an important area for massage, as the skull encases the brain, which is the seat of intelligence, knowledge, wisdom and power. Traditionally, yogis strive to make the body a fit vehicle for the spirit by the practice of asanas (postures). The yogic headstand (sirsasana) is known as the 'king of asanas', indicating the importance placed on the head area.

Indian Head Massage techniques have evolved from a rich tradition of family grooming practised in India for over 1000 years. The word 'shampoo' comes from the Hindi word for 'champi' meaning 'head massage'. In the Punjab region of India, head massage is known as 'malish'. Over generations, Indian women have been taught by their mothers to massage the head with different oils such as almond, coconut, mustard, olive and sesame to keep their hair strong, lustrous and in beautiful condition. Some oils, such as sesame, have the added benefit of being a natural sunscreen, filtering out up to 25 per cent of the sun's harmful rays. Oils are used according to the season, e.g. mustard oil in winter for its warming and stimulating properties (particularly in Northern India) and coconut in spring and summer for its cooling effects.

Royalty and other wealthy people often had their own personal head masseurs and it is speculated that these masseurs often acted as spies, selling secrets gleaned from the master as he relaxed into the soporific state that can often result from a head massage. Similarly, it is very easy for us to tell our deepest secrets to a hairdresser we have never met before as they manipulate our hair and scalp during a hairdressing session!

Head massage can be seen in India today – performed on street corners, markets, the beach and in family homes. In India it is common for barbers to provide head massage with a haircut or even with a wet shave.

The yogic headstand has many health benefits

Indian Head Massage as a complementary therapy

The popularity of Indian Head Massage as a complementary therapy in the West is largely due to the efforts of Narendra Mehta. He grew up in India with head massage as part of his daily life and when he moved to the UK in the 1970s he noticed this was a greatly neglected area within massage, even being omitted from a full body massage. He returned to India in 1979 and studied head massage across all the Indian traditions, arriving at these conclusions:

- ✎ By including the face, neck, shoulders and uppers arms (which are the most vulnerable areas for the accumulation of stress and tension) the benefits of a treatment were greatly enhanced.

- ✎ By introducing the Ayurvedic element of chakra balancing to the treatment in addition to massage, the subtle energy system could be positively affected.

- ✎ By using techniques that could be done as a 'dry' massage, without the need for clients to undress, the therapy would be accessible and convenient to those who may otherwise not have massage. The use of oil is an optional extra that can be performed at the end of a treatment.

Narendra Mehta introduced Indian Head Massage to the UK in 1981

Narendra Mehta introduced Indian Head Massage to the UK in 1981. Since then, its popularity has spread around the world.

casestudy

Therapist Vandana, who was brought up in Bombay, writes:

'I have fond memories of head massage in my family home where it was an important tradition. Throughout my childhood, until the age of 16, my mother would give me and my sister a weekly head massage using coconut oil. Afterwards she would plait our hair to "make the hair grow strong". We always left the oil on overnight, and after washing our hair the following day, it would be soft and shiny.

I also vividly remember a song from an old movie. The song is called "Champi Tel Malish", meaning "head massage with oil" – shortened simply to "champi" in India. A scene in the movie features a character wandering the streets singing a song encouraging people to have head massage. It is a very catchy song in Hindi and still popular in India today. I have translated some of the words:

When your head is spinning or your heart is sinking

Come my dear, come to me

Why fear, why fear!

Listen, listen, listen, oh my child, listen!

This champi has many good qualities

One medicine for plenty, and millions of sorrows

Why not try it

My oil is very exotic

Many, many people, their fate shone.

My mother once went to a fancy dress party dressed as the character in this film and sang his song. She won first prize!'

FAQs

What is Indian Champissage?

Champissage comes from the Hindi word 'champi', meaning 'massage of the head.' This is the name given to the Indian Head Massage therapy developed by Narendra Mehta, founder of the London Centre of Indian Champissage International. In its contemporary form, it is a massage of the upper back, shoulders, upper arms, neck, scalp, ears and face, together with energy balancing. The recipient is seated and remains fully clothed. The average length of a treatment is thirty minutes.

There seem to be many different ways of performing Indian Head Massage – is there one correct way?

Since Indian Head Massage was introduced to the West, techniques have been developed and adapted. The same therapist may also adapt their treatment to suit the individual client; for example avoiding certain areas of the body that are injured, adapting the pressure of the massage or concentrating more on areas of specific tension. This is all part of the holistic approach, where the treatment is geared towards the needs of the individual at the time.

subtle energy

Ayurveda

Ayurveda is the art of healthy living to create harmony in daily life. The concept that we are capable of taking charge of our own health and healing is a most important Ayurvedic principle. Harmony between mind, body and spirit is seen as fundamental to living well, and wilfully allowing yourself to deteriorate is seen as a crime against wisdom ('prajnaparadha'). When we allow blockages to occur in our bodies or minds through poor diet or harmful thoughts and emotions, this stagnation ('ama') can cause ill health.

In Ayurveda, each person is seen as having their own unique natural beauty: comparison to others is seen as self-destructive. When a person is healthy, happy and at peace, their 'ojas' or inner bliss radiates. According to Ayurvedic principles, one of the simplest ways to achieve well-being is through breath or 'prana'. Deep breathing is encouraged to relieve tension and promote good health and vitality. This has many health benefits including stimulation of the lymphatic system, an important part of our immune system.

Doshas

According to Ayurveda, the human body and everything in the universe is made up of five elements – water, earth, fire, air and ether (space). Just as water makes up over 70 per cent of planet Earth, our bodies also contain

Can you find the five elements in this picture?

11

indian head massage in essence

over 70 per cent water, with the other elements present in somewhat similar proportions to that of our planet. From the five elements, three subtle energies arise. These are 'vata' (composed of air and ether), 'pitta' (composed of fire and water) and 'kapha' (composed of water and earth).

Ayurveda teaches that health and well-being come from a harmonious balance of vata, pitta and kapha energy. All life forms possess these three qualities. Each individual has their own blend of the three and usually has at least one element that tends to get out of balance more easily than the others; this is termed our 'dosha'. Dosha literally means 'fault' – it comes from 'dush', meaning error, and relates to the prefix 'dys', from Greek (as in 'dysfunctional').

The combination of doshas you are born with is called your 'prakriti' or original constitution. It includes inherited traits, individual characteristics and tendencies such as body frame, eye colour, digestive capacity and emotional balance. While it is common for people to have nearly equal proportions of the three or just one predominant dosha, most people have two doshas that are more or less equally dominant, with the remaining one less dominant. For good health and well-being to be maintained, the three doshas within you need to be in balance. That doesn't mean they need to be equal (unless you were born that way) but that you need to maintain your original doshic make-up throughout life as much as possible to maintain good health. Unfortunately, factors such as diet, lifestyle, climate, pollution, work, relationships and even the passage of time can cause one or more doshas in your prakriti to increase or decrease from its original level, creating 'vikriti' or imbalance. If this is not corrected, you can eventually lose good health.

Vata

Vata is in charge of all movement in the body and mind. The root 'va' means 'to spread' and everything that moves from a single molecule to a thought moves because of vata. Predominantly vata types are light and slender, creative, active, spontaneous, idealistic and quick thinking. When imbalanced they are prone to depression, worry and insomnia and tend to over-indulge. They are sensitive to cold, wind and environmental factors and usually have dry skin and thin, sparse, brittle hair. Emotional stability, warmth, consistent schedules, rest and meditation help to balance vata. With age, the vata element in everyone naturally increases, leading to dryer skin and hair.

Terms associated with vata are: dry, cold, light, windy, rough, mobile, subtle, clear and astringent. Oils for vata types (or conditions of high vata such as hyperactivity, insomnia, dryness or deficient tissues) include sesame, almond and olive. Relaxing massage is recommended.

Pitta

Pitta is in charge of all transformation in the body and represents heat, metabolism and energy production. Predominantly pitta types are fiery in character, of medium height and build, rational, warm, friendly, courageous, ambitious and focused, but can be judgmental and angry under duress. They tend to have warm, sometimes oily skin, burn easily and are prone to rashes, inflammation, broken capillaries, freckles and moles. Pitta people need to learn how to work constructively with their energy and take time to cool down and rest from activity.

Terms associated with pitta are: hot, pungent, penetrating, light, oily, moist, sharp, liquid, spreading and sour. Oils for pitta types (or conditions of high pitta such as excess heat or anger) include cooling oils such as coconut, sunflower or safflower. Massage can help release toxins and rebalance.

Kapha

Kapha is the stabilising influence in a living being. Kapha types are often large and easily accumulate weight, water or mucus, due to a slow metabolism. They are sensitive to cold, dampness and stagnant air and feel better in conditions of warmth, dryness and increased activity. Kapha types are usually physically strong and sound sleepers. They are calm and easy-going but decisive, nurturing, warm, jolly, and supportive. When imbalanced they tend to become lazy, lethargic, possessive, depressed and set in their ways. Activity and exercise, avoidance of heavy foods and variation of routine help to balance excess kapha.

Terms associated with kapha are: heavy, mucous, oily, moist, cold, stable, smooth and soft. Oils for kapha types (or conditions of high kapha such as heaviness, excess tissue fluids or mucus) include a lighter application of warming oils such as mustard or apricot. Vigorous massage is recommended.

Determining the constitution

Proper hygiene, diet and lifestyle are essential prerequisites for good health and Ayurvedic treatments are always tailored to the individual in question. The starting point is to determine your constitution, which you can do by completing the questionnaire on pages 14 and 15.

Read the descriptions in the three columns one by one, across the page. Because dosha is fixed from conception, look at the tendencies that have persisted since childhood. Place a tick by the description that, of the three, best fits you. Then go on to the next line. When you have gone through all the lines, add up your ticks in each column to discover your dosha.

Aura and chakras

Working with subtle energy plays an important role in Ayurvedic healing. Indian Head Massage techniques harmonise subtle energy in three ways – through massage, chakra balancing and marma points. To harmonise subtle energy can help individuals realise their highest potential.

The aura

Every living thing – whether plant, animal or human – has its own subtle energy co-existing with the physical. The energy field permeating and surrounding living things is known as the 'aura'. Energy within the aura is given different names in different cultures (e.g. 'chi' in China, 'ki' in Japan and 'prana' in India). In the West

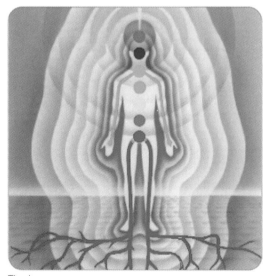

The human aura

indian head massage in essence

QUESTIONAIRE – Discover your DOSHA

Put a tick beside ANY of the following that apply to you in each section

	VATA	PITTA	KAPHA
HEIGHT	Very short, or tall and thin	Medium	Tall or short and sturdy
MUSCULAR	Thin, prominent tendons	Medium/firm	Plentiful/solid
BODY FRAME	Small frame	Medium frame	Large/broad
WEIGHT	Light, hard to gain	Medium weight	Heavy, gains easily
SWEAT	Minimal	Profuse, especially when hot	Moderate
SKIN	Dry, cold, rough, thin	Soft, warm, oily	Moist, cool, thick, possibly oily
COMPLEXION	Darkish	Fair, pink, red, freckles	Pale, white
HAIR AMOUNT	Average amount	Early thinning and greying	Plentiful
TYPE OF HAIR	Dry, thin, dark, coarse	Fine, soft, red, fair, oily	Thick, lustrous, brown, wavy, oily
SIZE OF EYES	Small, narrow or sunken	Average	Large, prominent
TYPE OF EYES	Dark brown or grey, dull	Blue / grey / hazel, intense	Blue, brown, attractive
TEETH AND GUMS	Crooked, receding gums	Moderate, gums bleed	White teeth, strong gums
SIZE OF TEETH	Small or large, irregular	Average	Large
PHYSICAL ACTIVITY	Moves quickly, active	Moderate pace, average	Slow pace, steady
ENDURANCE	Low	Good	Very good
STRENGTH	Poor	Good	Very good
TEMPERATURE	Dislikes cold, likes warmth	Likes coolness	Aversion to cool and damp
STOOLS	Tendency to constipation	Tendency to loose stools	Plentiful, slow elimination
LIFESTYLE	Variable, erratic	Busy, tends to achieve a lot	Steady, can skip meals
SLEEP	Light, interrupted, fitful	Sound, short	Deep, likes plenty
EMOTIONAL TENDENCY	Fearful, anxious, insecure	Fiery, angry, judgmental	Greedy, possessive

subtle energy

MENTAL ACTIVITY	Restless, lots of ideas	Sharp, precise, logical	Calm, steady, stable
MEMORY	Good recent memory	Sharp, generally good	Good long term
REACTION TO STRESS	Excites very easily	Quick temper	Not easily irritated
WORK	Creative	Intellectual	Caring
MOODS	Change quickly	Change slowly	Generally steady
SPEECH	Fast	Clear, sharp, precise	Deep, slow
APPETITE	Variable, nervous	High, excessive	Moderate but constant
THIRST	Low, scanty	High	Moderate
Totals: Add up each section to discover your dosha.	**VATA**	**PITTA**	**KAPHA**

it is known as the 'life-force', as it is said to be the universal energy sustaining all living things. The aura is depicted in ancient rock paintings, Christian icons and Indian art as a glow surrounding the whole body or a halo around the head. The size, shape and colours of individual auras vary, depending on the level of a person's evolvement. The aura is visible to clairvoyants as a luminous mist interpenetrating the body and extending beyond it.

The chakras

Chakras are energy centres within the aura, each chakra forming a layer that reflects aspects of being. The earliest known mention of chakras is found in the Upanishads, ancient Vedic texts dating back around 4000 years that primarily discuss meditation and philosophy. Chakra philosophy plays an important role in Hinduism and other Asian cultures, and more recently has been embraced in Western cultures by the New Age movement.

The word chakra comes from the Sanskrit 'cakra' meaning 'wheel' and is sometimes referred to as 'wheel of light/life', which conveys the idea of spinning energy, as chakra energy is said to flow in ceaseless movement. Male and female chakra points spin in opposite directions, enabling these energies to complement each other.

Traditional texts refer to seven main chakras, although emerging thought in the New Age movement refers to an awareness of twelve main chakras, reflecting man's evolvement. The seven main chakras emanate from the spine – from the base of the spine to the crown of the head. Secondary chakras are located around the body (e.g. on the palms and soles). Each chakra has a distinct vibration, increasing in intensity from the slower, denser vibration of the root chakra, to the higher, faster vibration of the crown.

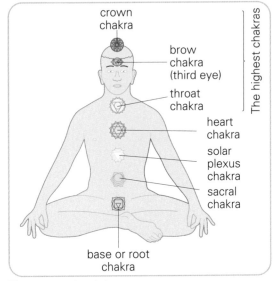

The seven major chakras

Although each chakra has several colours, one colour tends to dominate.

Chakras are considered sites of life energy ('prana') and their main function is to draw in prana to vitalise the spiritual, mental, emotional and physical aspects of man. It is thought that man needs three sources of energy for survival – food/water, air and prana. Each chakra relates to a particular area of human experience, from our basic survival to our highest aspirations, and they interact with the body through the endocrine and nervous systems. Each one is related to an organ, a gland, and a unique area of human experience and also has an element, a mantra (sound) and a colour associated with it.

In optimum health, chakra colours are clear and transparent. They are dynamic and constantly changing, becoming cloudy and darkened by disease and other factors including accidents, trauma, drugs and negative thoughts; and becoming clearer and vitalised in response to healing modalities, positive thoughts and healthy diet. An imbalance in one chakra will have a knock-on effect on other chakras and the disharmony

The seven major chakras

	Chakra	Element	Colour	Mantra	Physical body	Human experience
1	Muladhara (base)	Earth	Red	LAM	Spine, bones, kidneys, adrenals	Survival, security, confidence, strength
2	Savadhisthana (sacral)	Water	Orange	VAM	Ovaries, testes, prostate, uterus, bladder	Sexual energy, emotions
3	Manipura (solar plexus)	Fire	Yellow	RAM	Liver, digestive system, pancreas	Power, wisdom
4	Anahata (heart)	Air	Green/pink	YAM	Heart, thymus, immune system	Love, compassion
5	Vishudda (throat)	Ether	Blue	HAM	Lungs, throat, thyroid, parathyroids, hypothalamus	Communication, creativity, self-expression
6	Ajna (third eye)	Mind	Indigo	OM	Brain, pituitary	Intuition, knowledge
7	Sahasrara (crown)	Spirit	Violet/white /gold	OM	Brain, pineal	Spiritual aspiration

can eventually lead to disease in the physical body. Ayurvedic practices such as massage, yoga and meditation aim to harmonise subtle energy and prevent disease.

The chakra balancing techniques in Indian Head Massage use colour and sound to promote harmony to chakra energy. As the focus of treatment is on the upper body, the three higher chakras are worked on. This is very appropriate to the modern age, as we tend to live very much on an emotional/mental level – energies involving the upper three chakras. The crown chakra is the master chakra, ruling over prana as a whole, so to promote balance here is thought to harmonise all the chakras, in turn promoting healing on all levels. The table on page 18 lists some of the emotional and physical qualities that indicate when a chakra is in or out of balance.

In Indian tradition there is much symbolism associated with each chakra to emphasise its character, such as deities, planets and elements. One important symbol is the lotus flower, which like a water lily has its roots deep in mud

and darkness, but its flower blooms in the sunlight on the water's surface, representing

Indian deity with elaborate head-dress

Balanced and imbalanced chakras

Chakra	In balance	Out of balance
Muladhara (base)	Satisfaction, stability, inner strength, easy to achieve goals, accept life with gratitude	Feeling ungrounded, fearful; weakness in kidneys, legs, hips, buttocks
Svadisthana (sacral)	Ease and openness towards others, especially opposite sex; behave naturally	Possessiveness; sexual, reproductive, bowel or bladder disorders
Manipura (solar plexus)	Self-acceptance, inner harmony, respect for feelings and character traits of others	Anger, resentment, unworthiness, guilt; digestive disorders
Anahata (heart)	Radiate natural warmth, sincerity and happiness; inspire confidence and create joy	Unable to give or receive love, easily hurt; circulatory and immune disorders
Vishudda (throat)	Express feelings and thoughts freely and without fear; can also remain silent and listen with understanding	Frustration, inability to relax or express true feelings; disorders of throat and lungs
Ajna (third eye)	Active mind, advanced intellectual skills, ability to see beyond the world of appearances, intuitive	Hormonal imbalances, nightmares, headaches, sinus problems, dizziness, confusion, depression, eye disorders, diseases of the autonomic nervous system
Sahasrara (crown)	Experience of real Self as being part of an omnipresent pure energy, experience of bliss	Inability to make decisions, feeling isolated, fear of spiritual potential, unable to face reality; psychotic disorders

man's journey through life. Some astrologers consider that cosmic, planetary and zodiacal energies influence aspects of man via the chakras.

The chakras resemble funnel-shaped blossoms, each with a different number of petals, symbolising spokes of energy, the base chakra having the least and the crown chakra the most. The crown chakra is often referred to as 'the thousand-petalled lotus' and Indian art often depicts deities with elaborate head-dresses, fashioned to represent a highly evolved being with a well-developed crown chakra.

Marmas

Just as the physical body has a vital network of nerves centralised in the spinal column, the subtle body has a network of energy channels called meridians or nadis (from Sanskrit meaning 'channel', or 'flow'). There are 14 principal nadis, branching out to thousands of nadis, interconnecting the chakras. The use of pressure points is widespread tool in natural health-care, for example in acupressure. In Ayurveda these points are called 'marmas', meaning 'vulnerable' or 'sensitive' zones, and they are an important aspect of Ayurvedic treatments. Marmas connect to the nadis and chakras, and distribute prana throughout the body.

A marma point is a junction on the body where two or more types of tissue meet, for example muscles, veins, ligaments, bones or joints. There are 107 marma points throughout the body, with 37 located on the head and neck. They are measured by finger widths ('anguli') of the person being treated. The location may vary from one to eight finger widths, and often relates to a region rather than a specific point.

Just as acupuncture points are used in both Chinese medicine and martial arts, marma points are also used in the martial arts of India. Warriors learn how to strike these 'lethal' points with force and precision to fend off attackers. The Ayurvedic healthcare system uses 'therapeutic' marma points as a routine part of its preventative medicine. A professional therapist uses these points to balance the vital life-force for healing purposes. They also aim to tone the surrounding muscles and balance the doshas. By making gentle circular movements with the thumb, forefinger or middle finger on a marma point, toxins can be released and eliminated by the body. Movements are generally clockwise when toning or strengthening organs or tissues and counter-clockwise when reducing excess doshas or detoxifying. Marmas can be intentionally 'blocked' by pressing or holding the point to briefly allow the energy or circulating fluids to flow around the marma. Marmas are sensitive areas so massage should be done carefully. In some particularly vulnerable regions, such as the front of the neck, a gentle touch to convey prana is all that is required.

In Indian Head Massage, marmas are used to harmonise the flow of prana, or to treat a specific organ or system or a specific dosha imbalance. Oils are commonly applied to marma points on the head during the scalp massage. The head and neck have the largest number of marmas and these are important for treating psychological conditions and nervous system disorders.

The 14 regions and 37 marmas of the head and neck

Marma	Location		Meaning	Controls/Treats
Nila Size (anguli): 4 Number: 2 (1 on each side)	On internal jugular veins each side of neck, close to larynx		Dark blue	Speech, the thyroid, circulation from the brain
Manya Size (anguli): 4 Number: 2 (1 on each side)	Down and behind angle of mandible on each side		Honour	Circulatory system, tongue and salivation

Regions and marmas of the head and neck (continued)

Marma	Location		Meaning	Controls/Treats
Sira Matrika Size (anguli): 4 Number: 8 (4 on each side)	Each side of the neck, slightly higher than Nila (where carotid pulse is felt)		Mother of blood vessels	Blood flow from the heart to the brain and the nervous system
Phana Size (anguli): 1/2 Number: 2 (1 on each side)	Side of nostrils, with additional points located along the sides of the nasal bones		A serpent's hood	Sense of smell, nasal passages and sinuses
Apanga	On the outer corner of each eye		Outer corner of the eyes	Sense of sight (good marma to treat for photophobic headaches or sinusitis)
Vidhura Size (anguli): 1/2 Number: 2 (1 on each side)	Behind and below each ear, inferior to the mastoid process		'Distress' – due to its sensitive nature	Hearing (gentle acupressure here is good for clearing congestion from the ears)
Krikatika Size (anguli): 1/2 Number: 2 (1 on each side)	Junction of the head and neck		Joint of the neck	Body posture and circulation to the head (can be massaged firmly to relieve muscular tension)
Shanka Size (anguli): 1/2 Number: 2 (1 on each side)	On each temple between the top of the ear and lateral corner of the eye		A conch shell	Touch and gentle massage here is good for directing energy to the brain and mind
Utkshepa Size (anguli): 1/2 Number: 2 (1 on each side)	On the temporal arteries, just above the ears		What is upwards	Vata and the mind, large intestine and sense of smell (very gentle acupressure helps calm the mind and control vata)

Regions and marmas of the head and neck (continued)

Marma	Location		Meaning	Controls/Treats
Avarta Size (anguli): 1/2 Number: 2 (1 on each side)	Midpoint above the eyes		'Calamity' as it is very sensitive	Vata in general, sense of sight and bodily posture (should be massaged gently)
Shrinhataka Size (anguli): 4 Number: 4	Soft palate of the mouth, with a corresponding region on the face near the zygomatic arch		Place where 'four roads meet'	Diseases of the mouth (corresponding region on the face is treated)
Staphani Size (anguli): 1/2 Number: 1	Between the eyebrows (third eye)		What supports or fixes	Sixth chakra, prana, the mind, senses and pituitary gland (good point for acupressure to calm and focus the mind)
Simanta Size (anguli): 4 Number: 5	Along the sutures of the skull and covering a large area on the head		The summit	Crown chakra, nervous and circulatory systems, the mind and prana (massage well with fingers and palms and go over all skull sutures)
Adhipati Size (anguli): 1/2 Number: 1	Top of the skull (this is the soft spot on a baby's head)		The Lord of all	Crown chakra rules over prana as a whole (massage strongly for 5 minutes to calm mind and emotions and open up higher perceptive powers)

FAQs

I am concerned that if I work with chakra energy this will conflict with my religious beliefs. Can I leave out chakra balancing?

The principle of chakra energy is not to do with religious doctrine, and many therapists across the religious spectrum work with chakra energy. The idea of working with chakra energy in Indian Head Massage is to add a healing element to the treatment, so it is more than a mechanical massage. If you are not comfortable working with the chakras, then you could omit this part of the treatment or use your own form of healing instead – perhaps in the form of prayer or reiki (see Chapter 9).

How can I learn to feel subtle energy?

As an experiment, clench both your fists and place them next to each other; then vigorously rub the backs of your fingers back and forth for a minute. Unclench your fists and face your palms toward each other a few inches apart. You may feel a ball of energy between your palms and this sensation is subtle energy.

On entering certain places such as a dark, spooky house, a hospital, a prison, or a crowded bus, you can sometimes sense negative feelings or vibrations. Hiking in the mountains, listening to the waves on the seashore, reading uplifting poetry or scriptures, you can feel elated. The presence of certain people drains your energy, while others leave you feeling uplifted. These are all indications of subtle energy, so you are probably aware of it already but don't realise it!

When I did chakra balancing on my client she could see colours. Can you explain this?

Students and therapists often report this experience. The colours that clients see are sometimes colours that the therapist is visualising or colours of chakras that may be out of balance. Seeing colours usually indicates that the client is relaxed and open, and the balancing of their subtle energy is working in a highly effective way. When you are working in a healing way, energy seems to move to where it is most needed in the body. Clients will often feel heat from a therapist's hands during chakra balancing, usually indicating a high level of healing energy.

casestudy

This client experienced subtle energy changes during Indian Head Massage treatments.

Carolyn treated Fiona, aged 39, who presented with an extensive medical history including the removal of one ovary following the discovery of a non-malignant tumour three years previously. Fiona appeared to have a busy life with two teenage children, her own business and a full social life. To manage stress she drank wine in the evenings. She was craving junk food and chocolate and was a little overweight.

On her first visit, Fiona was feeling slightly depressed and fatigued and reported hair loss, possibly related to her past medical history. She experienced hot flushes at the start of treatment followed by excessive urination afterwards (which continued during the following days). Her hair appeared fine and tended to fall out easily during treatment, so Ayurvedic oil was applied to strengthen and nourish the scalp.

As treatments progressed Fiona opened up both physically and emotionally, experiencing energy shifts in the form of visualised colour (orange and blue in early treatments, red and white in later ones). She also experienced temperature changes throughout her body during treatment. By the third treatment she felt more grounded and centred.

Fiona reported a range of energetic changes during the five weeks of treatment, including tearfulness and blemishes around the mouth (possibly related to shifts in hormonal balance). Most surprising was her inability to drink alcohol – her body simply didn't want it. By the fourth treatment she was no longer craving junk food or chocolate, preferring healthy food options and water even at social events. As well as losing a stone and a half in weight, Fiona felt relaxed and better able to cope with stress. By the end of her course of treatments, she appeared fresh and alert. The results were quite remarkable.

the benefits of indian head massage

chapter 3

Indian Head Massage has evolved into a popular therapy that is very appropriate to our modern age. A typical treatment includes massage of the upper body – face, ears, shoulders, arms, neck and scalp – and includes chakra balancing and massage of marma points. A professional Indian Head Massage can have a profound effect on the whole body and mind, as there are many important energy points on the head.

What makes Indian Head Massage unique is that it is short, convenient, accessible and effective:

- Minimal equipment is required, making it highly mobile (i.e. therapists can travel to clients).
- The massage itself is usually done as a 'dry' massage with no need for oils or undressing, making it highly accessible.
- It is quick and easy to perform – a full treatment takes 30 minutes, but can be done in 15–20 minutes, making it ideal for clients who are 'short of time' (it is often described as a 'quick stress buster').
- The upper body is vulnerable to stress and tension, so massaging this area brings relief from many common conditions.
- The inclusion of chakra balancing and marma points balances subtle energy and promotes healing.
- The optional use of oil at the end of a treatment additionally benefits scalp and hair conditions.

Many businesses are discovering the benefits of Indian Head Massage, offering employees in-office treatments in the quest to combat stress, increase productivity and reduce absenteeism.

25

Benefits to body and mind

Indian Head Massage has numerous physical and psychological benefits.

Physical benefits

Indian Head Massage:

- ✒ encourages desquamation of skin cells and increases sebum production, helping to moisturise hair and improve the skin's elasticity and resistance to infection
- ✒ increases joint mobility and flexibility in shoulders, neck and arms by helping to free adhesions and break down scar tissue (as a result, it can improve range of motion in stiff joints and aid postural problems)
- ✒ reduces tension, stretches the tissues and increases flexibility in tense or overworked muscles and helps prevent stress-induced muscle spasm
- ✒ increases circulation of blood and lymph, improving delivery of nutrients and oxygen, speeding up waste removal and reducing swelling (oedema) caused by excess fluid in tissues
- ✒ improves nutrition to cells, helping to reduce hair loss, premature balding and greying
- ✒ improves circulation, helping to remove lactic acid from muscles, reducing aches and soreness
- ✒ decreases heart rate, lowers blood pressure and dilates blood vessels, helping them work more efficiently
- ✒ boosts the immune system through improved production and delivery of white blood cells
- ✒ relieves problems such as sinusitis and nasal congestion in the upper respiratory system

- ✒ stimulates the parasympathetic nervous system, which reduces the effects of stress, facilitates sleep, reduces anxiety, slows heart rate, improves breathing, releases physical and mental tension and promotes feelings of calmness and well-being
- ✒ can stimulate or relax the nervous system, depending on goal of treatment and techniques used
- ✒ clears the mind and revitalises mental capacity, improving alertness, concentration and productivity
- ✒ stimulates the release of endorphins, which reduce pain and elevate the mood
- ✒ increases levels of hormones such as oxytocin, which have a positive effect on mood and behaviour, and balances the release of stress hormones from adrenal glands
- ✒ increases blood flow to digestive, urinary and reproductive systems, which receive a reduced blood supply in times of stress – this can relieve stress-related digestive

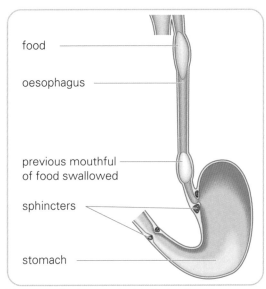

food

oesophagus

previous mouthful of food swallowed

sphincters

stomach

Massage stimulates peristalsis in the digestive system

disorders such as irritable bowel syndrome, increase urinary output and elimination of waste and improve function of the reproductive organs.

Psychological benefits

Indian Head Massage:

- ℞ reduces stress and anxiety by relaxing the mind and body
- ℞ creates a feeling of well-being and enhanced self-esteem

- ℞ eases emotional trauma through relaxation – this can lead to an emotional release and occasionally tears.

Effects on subtle energy

Indian Head Massage also has a general 'balancing' effect, giving a sense of calmness and peace. It works on balancing the chakras and releases stagnant energy so the body can function more harmoniously. (See Chapter 2 for more information.)

Common ailments that can benefit from Indian Head Massage

The following conditions can benefit from Indian Head Massage. However, precautions, adaptations, recommendations or referrals will be necessary in treating clients with some of these conditions.

Alopecia

This is sudden and severe hair loss, usually due to stress, shock, illness, chemotherapy or sometimes pregnancy. It is also thought to be an auto-immune condition. Hair loss is temporary and should not be confused with male-pattern baldness, where hair loss is permanent. Bald patches are random and sometimes red and scaly. There are three types of alopecia:

1 alopecia areata causes hair to be lost in patches

2 alopecia totalis is total loss of hair from the head

3 alopecia universalis is total loss of all head and body hair.

Note – *A treatment including oil helps a client to relax, which can lessen the effects of the problem, condition the scalp and stimulate hair growth. Clients should be encouraged to massage their scalp between treatments.*

Alopecia

casestudy

Mary, who has suffered from intermittent alopecia areata for over twenty years, tells her story:

'One day while walking down stairs a friend commented from above that I had a bald patch on top of my head – I thought she was joking as my hair was long and thick. I looked in a mirror and saw she was right – an area the size of a ten pence coin was smooth and hairless. Horrified, I saw my doctor who diagnosed 'alopecia areata'. He explained the different types, and suggested mine was probably stress-related. He prescribed medication to apply daily as I massaged my scalp, and advised that more stress could worsen the condition. After diagnosis, more bald patches appeared and it was difficult not to worry about it. I improved my diet, had regular head massage and took recommended nutritional supplements. After about a year the hair slowly began to grow back. That was over twenty years ago and since then the condition has struck several times, usually when I am under a lot of stress. I don't worry about it any more as I know the hair will grow back eventually. It has made me take more care with my lifestyle and nutrition.'

Dandruff

Dandruff is a term for all types of scalp flaking and is the most common condition affecting the scalp. The cells on our scalp constantly renew and dead cells are normally brushed or washed off without being noticed. With dandruff, this process is speeded up so more cells are shed and these clump together and become visible. Pityriasis capitis is the most common form of dandruff. Flakes of skin can be seen in the hair and on the shoulders. The flakes are greyish-white and the scalp may feel tight, itchy and sore. A more severe form of oily dandruff due to excess sebum, called seborrhoeic dermatitis or seborrhoeic eczema, can affect skin on the face, ears and scalp.

Dandruff is caused when the skin reacts to a naturally occurring yeast fungus called 'pityrosporum ovale'. This yeast is normally kept in a dormant state by secretions of sweat and sebum. However, if these secretions change, the yeast can flourish – speeding up the skin-shedding process. Triggers are poor diet, dehydration, stress, hormonal imbalance or a reaction to hair products.

Note – *Indian Head Massage helps remove dead cells, loosen tight muscles and stimulate circulation. Using oil can provide an added benefit by conditioning the scalp.*

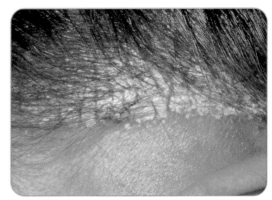

Dandruff is the most common condition to affect the scalp

Headaches

Headaches create a dull aching pain that affects one or both sides of the head. The head can feel as if compressed by a tight band and pain can spread to the back of the head and neck.

> Note – *Dehydration is a common cause of headaches. To maintain a healthy body it is recommended we drink between one and two litres of water per day. Many people drink little or none. Simply drinking more water can often alleviate headaches.*

Headaches are a common problem and have several causes – some chronic or recurrent, and others that are non-recurrent. Because there are so many possible causes of headache, each case must be treated individually.

Chronic or recurrent headaches

These include:

- migraines
- tension and muscular headaches
- a combination of migraine and tension
- headaches brought on by emotion, such as depression.

Migraines

Migraine is the name given to a type of headache that usually affects one half of the head and is most intense just above, or centred on, the eye on the painful side. Symptoms are severe and include nausea, disturbed vision and sensitivity to light. Sufferers often need to lie down in a darkened room. A bout of migraine can last for several days.

A study led by doctors in London and Shrewsbury (2006) has associated migraine with a tiny hole in the heart, known technically as a patent foramen ovale (PFO). This is a minor defect in the wall separating the two upper chambers of the heart. It is quite common and in most cases causes no health problems, but it is thought that failure to completely filter the blood of impurities in the normal way may result in migraines. Scientists found that surgical repair of the defect cut the severity of migraine attacks by 37 per cent.

The American Academy of Family Physicians (1996) suggests that changes in serotonin levels within the brain may play a part in the onset of migraines. When serotonin levels are high, blood vessels constrict; when levels fall, vessels dilate, causing swelling and pain. Serotonin levels are also linked to changes in the levels of blood sugar and oestrogen.

Tension is responsible for a high percentage of migraine and other headaches, but allergic reaction to certain foods or additives can also provoke headaches. The following substances can produce headaches in some individuals: chocolate, cheese and dairy products, fruit (particularly citrus), alcohol, fried and fatty foods, certain vegetables, tea and coffee, meat (especially pork), seafood.

> Note – *Indian Head Massage can be highly effective in relieving headaches and reducing the frequency and severity of migraines. The pain of some headaches, particularly migraines, can be made worse by physical activity, so massage is not recommended or not usually desired during an attack, but can be done if the headache is mild. Encourage clients who suffer from chronic or recurrent headaches to seek medical advice as it is important to identify the cause.*

casestudy

Linda describes treating Paula, aged 32, for migraines:

Paula suffered debilitating migraines on a regular basis with symptoms including severe pain in the head, face and neck, nausea and dizziness. During an attack she was unable to work, sometimes for two days. She started treatments as she was concerned she would suffer a migraine on her wedding day. The muscles in her shoulders and neck were extremely tight and those around her occipital bone were particularly tender during the first treatment. Her scalp muscles were also tight, particularly on the right side. She had treatments on a regular basis for eight weeks. As her treatments progressed, the severity and frequency of her migraines reduced significantly, and her muscles became looser and less tender. Paula was delighted with the results and had a happy, migraine-free wedding day.

Non-recurrent headaches

These include headaches that:

- have a vascular basis, i.e. raised blood pressure, anaemia, drugs or hormones
- are accompanied by fevers
- derive from anatomical structures (e.g. sinuses, stiff neck or shoulders, eyestrain, ear, teeth or jaw problems)
- follow injury
- have a neurological basis (e.g. tumours, infections, bleeding or clots, epilepsy, neuralgia).

Sinus problems

Sinus problems are common and can be debilitating. The sinuses are air-filled cavities around the nose and eyes, lined with mucus membranes. Mucus passes continuously through narrow channels leading from the sinuses to the nasal cavity. These passages can become blocked, leading to a build-up of mucus and inflammation of the sinuses. The most common cause is viral infection, such as the common cold. Sinusitis may be acute (developing and clearing rapidly) or chronic (long term). Symptoms include headache, feelings of congestion, and pain and tenderness in the face that tends to worsen on bending down.

> Note – *Indian Head Massage can relieve congestion in the sinuses by stimulating circulation and by massage of specific sinus points on the face. A reduction in dairy products can reduce the amount of mucus in the body.*

Stress

Dr Hans Seyle defined stress as 'the non-specific response of the body to any demands placed upon it'. Seyle, who popularised the word 'stress' in the 1950s, set up the International Institute of Stress in Montreal in 1977. He discovered that hormones released in response to stress participate in the development of many degenerative diseases. He also saw that when faced with demands, be they physical or emotional, people reacted in different ways and what was stressful for one person could be exciting and stimulating for another. Positive stress that motivates is defined as 'eustress' and we all need a certain amount of this in our lives in order to function well. Stress becomes harmful (distress) when it occurs too often or lasts too long. Fatigue is one of the first signs of distress and we need to do something about it before it becomes exhaustion and leads to ill health.

> Note – *Indian Head Massage is an ideal antidote to stress as it works on areas of the body that are particularly vulnerable to the effects of stress.*

casestudy

Caroline, a practitioner, describes treating Jane, aged 36, for stress and depression:

'Jane is a housewife who was finding life difficult. Her husband left his job and had been at home, feeling unsure about the future, which was very unsettling for Jane and their three children. She became very anxious and depressed and on one occasion felt so low she visited her GP, who prescribed antidepressants. In an effort to avoid long-term medication she came to me for a course of Indian Head Massage treatments.

Jane's initial five treatments were weekly. During the first treatment she felt like she was "inside a volcano and floating up to the opening where it was getting brighter". After treatment she felt relaxed, calm and her troubles seemed to dissipate. During the next week she felt less anxious and mentally tired. During the second treatment she again felt her troubles dissipate and described it as 'a wonderful feeling'. As each week and treatment passed she began to feel more in control of her life and more positive about the future. Each time the feeling of well-being and positive outlook was more prolonged. By treatment five, Jane was delighted with the results and returned the unopened packet of antidepressants to her doctor. Now (one year on) she is continuing a happy medication-free life, helped by regular treatments.'

Temporomandibular Joint (TMJ) syndrome

In this condition the temporomandibular joint does not function properly. This joint connects the temporal bone with the mandible and is frequently used – when we talk, chew, bite down or swallow we put the TMJ to work. TMJ syndrome produces pain in the jaw that can radiate to the face, neck, head and shoulders and there may be difficulty opening the mouth fully. Clicking and popping noises can occur when chewing, yawning, or moving the joint. It can contribute to headaches, migraines or tinnitus. The common causes are stress and a poor bite, combined with grinding the teeth, especially at night. Chewing gum can worsen the problem.

> Note – *This condition should be diagnosed and treated by a specialist. Indian Head Massage can alleviate stress and relax muscles in the area.*

Tinnitus

This is a condition in which the sufferer is conscious of a ringing, buzzing or tinkling noise in one or both ears that has no external source. One in ten people have it in a mild way. For one in 100 people it is bad enough to affect their quality of life. It is more common in older

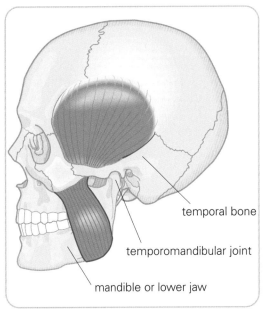

Temporomandibular joint

people, but can occur at any age. Causes include TMJ syndrome, high or low blood pressure, and ear disorders such as compacted earwax, deafness, inner- or middle-ear infections and Ménière's disease.

> Note – *Tight muscles in the head and neck or stress can trigger tinnitus and this can be relieved by Indian Head Massage. Ear candling also alleviates this condition.*

Bell's palsy

This is paralysis of the facial nerve (the seventh cranial nerve), causing weakness of muscles on one side of the face and an inability to close the eye. Causes include colds and chills, tumours, injury to the nerve, inner-ear infection, dental surgery, diabetes, pregnancy and hypertension. Most cases make a complete recovery.

> Note – *Gentle massage and facial exercises can help this condition, so long as it is not painful for the client to have their face touched.*

Torticollis

Torticollis, commonly known as 'wry neck', is a deformity of the neck in which the head tilts toward one shoulder and the chin rotates toward the opposite shoulder. Congenital muscular torticollis is the most common form and is usually diagnosed in the first months of life. It is associated with a benign tumour in the sternocleidomastoid muscle and affects the right side in 75 per cent of cases. There may be a soft lump in the belly of the muscle that generally disappears, and the muscle feels tight and shortened. The theory is that during delivery, blood-flow to the affected neck muscle is reduced, causing damage. Physiotherapy is successful in curing the problem.

A stiff neck or 'crick in the neck' is also termed torticollis. This is normally due to sudden movement, sleeping in a draught or an awkward position and can lead to intense pain and stiffness in the muscles of the neck on one side. Rest will usually cure the condition. Extreme cases may require muscle relaxant medication or a surgical collar.

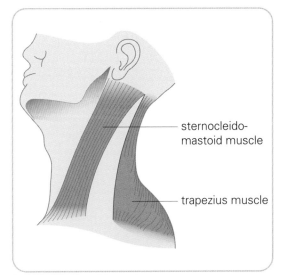

Sternocleidomastoid muscle

Note – *Gentle massage of the area can help. Refer the client to a doctor or osteopath if underlying problems such as injury to discs in the neck are indicated.*

Frozen shoulder (adhesive capsulitis)

The term 'frozen shoulder' is used to describe the condition when a shoulder becomes painful and immobilised. This condition arises if the shoulder is used incorrectly, becomes painful and the person avoids using it. Scar tissue develops that stops the shoulder moving. The shoulder may go through several stages as the scar tissue forms:

1 the painful stage, where the shoulder may ache, feel stiff and get very painful – this can last between three and eight months

2 the adhesive stage, where there may not be as much pain, but the shoulder keeps getting stiffer – this usually lasts between four and six months

3 the final recovery stage, which usually lasts between one and three months. The shoulder is not very painful but it becomes hard to move it even a little. After a while the stiffness slowly goes and the shoulder can be moved again.

As shoulder movement increases, there may still be pain at times. Sufferers usually regain full use of their shoulder, while others may always have a little stiffness and pain in that shoulder.

Note – *Massage can ease tension in muscles surrounding the shoulder joint but should not be done during the painful stage. Before massaging, ensure a medical practitioner has confirmed it is frozen shoulder and not a different problem. When medically diagnosed, exercises are recommended by the doctor or physiotherapist to help break up scar tissue*

Spondylitis

Spondylitis is chronic inflammation of the spine ('spondylos' is Greek for 'spine'). Ankylosing spondylitis is a chronic inflammation of the spine and sacroiliac joints which are located in the lower back where the sacrum (the bone directly above the tailbone) meets the iliac bones (the large bones of the pelvic girdle).

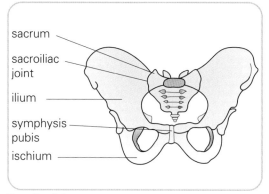

sacrum
sacroiliac joint
ilium
symphysis pubis
ischium

Sacroiliac joints

Chronic inflammation in these areas causes pain and stiffness in and around the spine. Over time, as inflammation subsides and healing takes place, bone grows out from both sides of the vertebrae and may lead to vertebrae fusing together – this stiffness, called 'ankylosis', leads to loss of spine mobility.

Ankylosing spondylitis is also a systemic rheumatic disease, meaning it can affect tissues throughout the body. It can cause inflammation or injury to other joints away from the spine, as well as to organs, such as eyes, heart, lungs and kidneys. The condition predominantly affects young males. Symptoms include low backache, pain in buttocks and thighs, chest pain from joints between ribs and sternum, inflammation of iris of eye (red pupil), colitis and psoriasis.

Spondylosis is non-inflammatory degenerative (wear and tear) of the spinal column, such as degenerative disc disease. The discs between the vertebrae become narrower and osteophytes (extra bone growth on the edges of vertebrae which cause narrowing of nerve canals) form at the junction of the disc and vertebra. This can lead to stiffness and eventually, fixation of the joint. Narrowing of nerve canals puts pressure on nerve roots, leading to pain and tingling sensations. It commonly affects the neck (cervical spondylosis) in older people.

Note – *Seek medical approval before treating anyone with these conditions. Avoid manipulating the neck as you may cause more damage. Ensure the client is comfortable during treatment.*

Osteoarthritis

'Osteo' means bone and 'arthritis' means joint damage and inflammation. This is the commonest form of joint disease, where there is damage to the surface of the joint and an abnormal reaction in the underlying bone. It is a degenerative disorder, most often affecting weight-bearing joints (knees and hips) and sometimes lumbar and cervical vertebrae. It can occur with ageing due to 'wear and tear', or prematurely, for reasons such as obesity (which places undue stress on weight bearing joints) or following injury to a joint. There is a breakdown of articular cartilage covering and cushioning the ends of bones within the joint and the bone surfaces rub against each other. The body attempts to repair the damage with an overgrowth of bone (bone spurs) that worsen the condition. Symptoms include pain (usually after prolonged activity), stiffness (particularly in the morning or with inactivity), loss of function, reduced joint motion, and deformity. Unlike rheumatoid arthritis, osteoarthritis does not result from inflammation.

Note – *Gentle massage can loosen muscles and provide overall relaxation. Avoid any manipulation of the neck if this region is affected. If knees or hips are affected, ensure that client is comfortable during treatment. Medical approval may be required.*

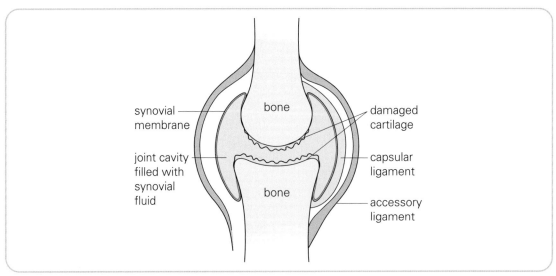

synovial membrane

bone

damaged cartilage

joint cavity filled with synovial fluid

capsular ligament

bone

accessory ligament

Joint with osteoarthritis

Fibromyalgia

This chronic condition primarily occurs in females and affects muscles and ligaments but does not damage joints. The fibrous tissues (fibro–) and muscles (–my) are affected by pain (–algia) and tenderness. It is characterised by widespread musculoskeletal pain, fatigue, and multiple tender points in precise localised areas, particularly the neck, spine, shoulders, and hips. It may also cause sleep disturbances, morning stiffness, irritable bowel syndrome, anxiety, and other symptoms. Many medical professionals believe there is a connection between fibromyalgia and chronic fatigue syndrome; some even theorise that they are actually the same.

Note – *Massage can help with associated stress and improve sleeping pattern. Avoid deep pressure on tender areas.*

Myalgic Encephalomyelitis (ME)

Also known as chronic fatigue syndrome or post-viral fatigue, this debilitating condition usually follows a viral infection. Its symptoms include extreme tiredness, weakness, muscle ache, joint pain, headache, stomach ache, lymph node pain, sore throat and depression. People with ME have memory problems and find it hard to concentrate. They tend to be sensitive to light, sound, some chemicals and foods. Neurological problems include dizziness and light-headedness, especially when standing up quickly. The condition is not due to exertion, is not alleviated by rest, and substantially reduces everyday activities.

Note – *Indian Head Massage can help with associated depression and anxiety. A relaxing treatment without deep pressure is recommended. A shorter treatment is more appropriate, as clients with ME may find a full treatment too exhausting.*

Whiplash

This is caused by a sudden, involuntary, forced movement of the head in any direction, with the rebound of the head or neck in the opposite direction. Consequently, there are injuries to the surrounding and supporting tissues of the neck and head. The commonest cause is a road traffic accident when the vehicle is shunted from behind. Headrests can reduce the risk of this injury occurring.

Note – *Recent whiplash injuries should not be treated until the client has had a full medical examination to ensure no vertebrae or discs are affected. With older injuries, gentle massage of the neck can ease pain and restore mobility, but avoid vigorous movements.*

the benefits of indian head massage

FAQs

Can Indian Head Massage benefit children as well as adults?

Most definitely. At the Touch Research Institute (TRI) in Miami, Florida, researchers examining the effects of touch demonstrated its anxiety-reducing, calming and relaxing effects on both children and adults. The TRI has conducted over 90 studies on the positive effects of touch therapy on many conditions, with the major cause for these improvements being decreased levels of stress hormones.

Infant massage is recognised throughout the world, mainly due to the work of the International Association of Infant Massage (IAIM). The Association was founded by Vimala McClure, who was inspired by the positive effects of massage she observed while working in an Indian orphanage.

Therapists have also developed massage approaches for individuals with special needs and young children in pre-school. Since 2002, a 'Massage in Schools Programme' has been running in many UK schools. This programme, originated by Mia Elmsater from Sweden and Sylvie Hetu from Canada, has reported numerous benefits, including calmer children, improved concentration and motor skills as well as a reduction in bullying and aggression. For address details, see the 'Where to go from here' section near the end of this book.

Can giving Indian Head Massage benefit the person giving the treatment?

In 1906, the English researcher Sir Henry Dale discovered a substance in the pituitary gland that could speed up the birthing process and promote the expression of breast milk. He named it oxytocin, from the Greek words for 'quick childbirth labour'. Oxytocin was later shown to play a role in relaxation as well as influencing many vital operations in the body. Older hospital patients who receive massage sleep better, experience less pain, need less medication and often become less confused and more sociable – probably due to increased oxytocin and endorphin levels. Although we normally associate this hormone with childbirth because it is produced in response to uterine contractions, both females and males have the same distribution of oxytocin-producing cells. It is possible to elevate levels of oxytocin with stimuli such as warmth, touch and massage. Studies show that the person administering 'touch' also experiences heightened levels of oxytocin. According to Kerstin Uvnas Moberg, author of *The Oxytocin Factor* (2003), many massage therapists exhibit the effects of high levels of oxytocin, such as lower levels of stress hormones and lowered blood pressure.

using oils in indian head massage

Many factors affect the growth and condition of hair, such as illness, diet, stress, medication and over-processing, and these are discussed in Chapter 8. Such factors can result in:

- thinning hair/baldness
- loss of hair colour
- hair that lacks shine
- dry, brittle, lifeless hair
- dry, itchy, flaky scalp
- skin conditions affecting the scalp, such as eczema.

Indian Head Massage techniques promote healthy hair by loosening scalp muscles, stimulating circulation and promoting relaxation. Many hair problems can be further alleviated by the use of oils. Oils are often applied at the end of an Indian Head Massage treatment. When oil is applied to the scalp it is absorbed into hair follicles, with the following benefits:

- lubricates, nourishes and softens the scalp
- relieves skin disorders affecting the scalp
- helps scalp problems such as dandruff and head lice

- stimulates hair growth
- hydrates and moisturises hair
- promotes vibrant, shiny hair
- some oils offer protection from UV rays.

When aromatic oils are used on the scalp, the molecules quickly reach the nose and this can relax the client further and promote deeper breathing. The use of oil is optional at the end of a treatment. It can be gently heated to open the pores, increase circulation and aid penetration.

Oils known as 'carrier oils' are extracted from vegetables, flowers, nuts or seeds and have therapeutic properties in their own right. For therapeutic use the oils should be cold-pressed and, where possible, organic. Oils are highly recommended within Ayurvedic medicine and have been used for centuries in Indian families to keep hair strong and shiny. These oils include sesame, almond, coconut, neem and mustard. Oils are often mixed with henna and essential oils such as sandalwood, lemon or rosemary and herbs that are less known in the West, for example brahmi, bringraj, shikakai and amla.

Carrier oils should be kept in airtight containers and stored in a cool, dark place to prolong their shelf life. Some carrier oils, particularly nut oils, can provoke allergic reactions so avoid using these on clients with a nut allergy. See the Bibliography for details of an article on the safety of nut oils and recommended alternatives (Buck and Bensouilah, 2005).

Traditional oils used in Indian Head Massage

Almond oil (Prunus amygdalus)

Description
Almond oil is derived from the kernels (nuts) of the almond tree, which flowers with a profusion of pink blossom. The almonds form on short branches and are protected by a tough outer husk, which later splits to reveal the nut inside. The almond tree is a native of the Middle East but now grows in the sunny climates of the Mediterranean and California. The Romans introduced almond oil to Britain and it has continued to be an important element of skincare throughout history. Almond oil is popular in India and also easily obtainable in the Western world.

Therapeutic use
The type of oil used in skin and hair preparations is cold- or warm-pressed from sweet almond kernels and usually referred to as 'sweet almond oil'. It is high in Vitamin E and fatty acids and has a delicate aroma. Almond oil benefits all skin types, particularly inflamed or irritated skin, dermatitis and psoriasis (common in the scalp), dry scalp and brittle hair. It is said to reduce muscular aches and pains and calm the nerves, making it suitable for excess vata.

Avoid in cases of nut allergy.

The sweet almond tree

Coconut oil (Cocos nucifera)

Description
This oil originates from the fruits of the hardy coconut palm that thrives on dry sandy soils such as those in the Philippines, Sri Lanka and India. Coconut palms are abundant in the Kerala region of Southern India, which is often referred to as 'the land of coconuts'. The Sanskirt name 'kalpa vriksha' means 'the tree that provides all necessities of life'. Pure coconut oil has a creamy-white colour, a waxy appearance and a distinct aroma. It is solid at room temperature and needs to be gently heated before use, either in the therapist's hands or placed in warm water, to liquefy the oil. The type of coconut oil most widely available in the West is referred to as 'fractionated', which is produced by heating the oil and removing the top liquid fraction. This results in odourless oil with a clear light texture that penetrates the skin well, making it suitable as base oil for aromatherapy and massage. Coconut oil is slow to oxidise and has a long shelf-life. Studies show the health benefits of using coconut oil in the diet.

Therapeutic use

According to Ayurvedic classics, coconut oil nourishes the body, increases strength and is reputed to reduce premature ageing. It is traditionally used in spring and is used commercially in skin and hair care products, as well as sunscreens. Its emollient qualities are excellent for moisturising skin and hair and it can relieve disorders such as psoriasis and dandruff. Its cooling nature is beneficial in cases of excess pitta. The use of coconut oil medicated with herbs is widespread in India. Different preparations of coconut oil promote luxurious hair growth and protect the skin from infections. For some head conditions, such as lice, an application of coconut oil medicated with palm roots is an effective treatment.

Coconut oil has cooling qualities

Mustard oil (Brassica juncea)
Description

Several varieties of mustard plant are grown around the world. Indian mustard originates from the foothills of the Himalayas. Seeds of the plant are pressed to extract the oil, which has a strong smell and a hot nutty taste and is widely used in Indian cookery. Mustard oil has a high content of erucic acid, which is considered noxious and some say 'not suitable for human consumption', although mustard oil with a low content of erucic acid is available.

Many Indians who have used mustard oil for years say that there is not enough evidence for the toxicity of erucic acid and continue using it with no apparent problems. Outside India, the oil is often sold 'for external use only' in stores catering to Indian immigrants, but it is not widely available.

Therapeutic use

In India, particularly in the northwest, mustard oil is commonly used for massage, including head massage. As it generates heat, it is useful in the cold winter months. Mustard oil is particularly favoured by males and is often used by wrestlers and bodybuilders in India. It stimulates circulation, reduces pain and swelling in conditions such as arthritis and soothes sore, tense muscles. Its warming and stimulating properties make it suitable for kapha types in Ayurvedic treatments. The strong scent of mustard oil may not appeal to everyone and as it can irritate the skin, it should be used with caution. It can be blended with other oils such as sesame or almond.

Mustard oil is traditionally used in winter

Neem oil (Azadirachta indica)
Description

Neem oil is pressed from the fruits and seeds of the neem, an evergreen tree found in abundance in southern India and now introduced to many other areas of the tropics. Its name in Sanskrit means 'reliever of sickness' and it is mentioned in ancient texts. Hindus consider the neem tree sacred and various parts are used in rituals and ceremonies. Neem oil is generally light to dark brown, bitter with a strong odour that has been compared to the mixed odours of peanut and garlic. The oil is obtained through crushing the seed kernels, either through cold pressing or through a process incorporating temperature controls. It can also be obtained by solvent extraction – this version is of a lower quality than the cold-pressed oil and is mostly used in soap manufacture.

Therapeutic use

Neem oil is used in India and Bangladesh for preparing cosmetics (soap, hair products, body and hand creams) and in the treatment of a wide range of conditions. Ancient Ayurvedic writings report its benefits in treating skin diseases, inflammation and fever, and more recently it has been used to treat rheumatic disorders and as an insect repellent. A few drops of neem oil mixed with sweet almond is a common treatment for head lice. Its anti-microbial quality makes it an excellent choice for hair problems, particularly stubborn dandruff and fungal infections such as ringworm. It can be blended with other oils to disguise its aroma.

Sesame oil (Sesamum indicum)
Description

The sesame plant is a leafy shrub with pinkish-white flowers. It requires several months of hot sunshine to ripen the seedpods, which yield the oil-laden seeds. This is the most widely used oil in India, particularly in the west, and one of the oldest seed oils known to mankind. The sesame plant was cultivated 4000 years ago in Mesopotamia, an area of the world located between the Tigris and Euphrates rivers, most of which is now Iraq. It is widely grown in tropical regions of Africa, India, Pakistan and Sri Lanka. The seeds are rich in calcium, potassium, manganese and copper, and contain Vitamin B1 and Vitamin E. They also contain powerful antioxidants called lignans, which are said to help prevent cancers, as well as phytosterols, which block cholesterol production.

Therapeutic use

Sesame oil – particularly oil extracted from black sesame seeds – is highly recommended within Ayurvedic medicine and is one of the most popular oils in India for therapeutic use. It is light and easily absorbed with little aroma,

Oil from the neem tree has many therapeutic uses

Sesame oil is traditionally used in summer for its sun-screening properties

making it ideal for all forms of massage. Toasted sesame oil used in stir-fry cooking, which has a strong aroma, is not suitable for therapeutic use. Ayurveda views sesame oil as the most beneficial for treating dry skin and other health problems associated with excess vata. It is said to slow down premature ageing and greying of the hair and to penetrate the deeper layers of the skin, calming nerves, and reducing muscular aches, pains, swelling and stiffness. A few drops massaged into the soles of the feet at night can promote sleep. Sesame oil is traditionally used in summer as it offers some protection from UV rays. Avoid in cases of nut allergy.

casestudy

Gina discovered that besides its benefits in Indian Head Massage, sesame oil has many therapeutic uses.

'During a recent Indian Head Massage class, the use of oils was discussed. I was fascinated by the many therapeutic uses of sesame oil and eager to find out more. I searched the internet and found information about the use of sesame oil to treat bleeding gums. I have recently been suffering with bleeding gums so I followed these instructions:

- Swish about 15mls of sesame oil around the mouth for 10–15 minutes or until the golden oil turns white.

The reason it turns white is because it has drawn out toxins, so try not to swallow any.

- Spit out the now white oil, rinse your mouth with warm water and brush teeth as normal.

- Do this morning and evening.

I have only been doing this for a few days and find it incredible. My gums have stopped bleeding. Apparently it whitens teeth as well! You must use organic, cold-pressed sesame oil and store it in a dark glass bottle, as light can ruin the quality.'

Other oils used in the West

Apricot kernel (Prunus armenaica)

Description
The apricot tree originates from the Himalayas and other parts of temperate Asia and is now grown in many regions of Europe and other parts of the world. It is a small, hardy tree with an abundance of white flowers, tinged with dusky red, that appear in early spring. The oil is extracted by pressing the seed kernel of its juicy fruit, the apricot. The oil is clear, slightly yellow, light and easily absorbed. It is high in polyunsaturated fatty acids and vitamins A and C.

Therapeutic use
The light texture of apricot kernel oil makes it a popular choice for massage. It benefits all skin types but is especially recommended for dry, sensitive, mature or ageing skin. It relieves the itching and swelling associated with eczema and is excellent for face and head massage.

The apricot tree

Evening primrose oil can help with eczema and psoriasis

Evening primrose (Oenothera biennis)

Description

This oil derives from a tall, spiky plant with delicately fragranced, yellow flowers that open only in the evening. The evening primrose originates from North America and its seedpods and roots were used by North American Indians to make a salve to heal wounds and a poultice to ease aches and pains. It was also used by the Romans and has been the subject of scientific study for over 100 years. It contains a valuable fatty acid called gamma linoleic acid (GLA) that aids many important body functions.

Therapeutic use

Evening primrose capsules are used to treat a variety of conditions, and the oil is widely used commercially in skin and hair products. In massage, the oil helps to balance sebum secretions and is suitable for all skin types. It has mild anti-inflammatory actions and is used for dry, devitalised skin and mild forms eczema and psoriasis. As it is expensive, it can be blended with other oils.

Grapeseed (Vitis vinifera)

Description

The cultivation of vines goes back to the origins of man and the use of grapes in cosmetics dates to at least the seventeenth century. Grapeseed oil is a by-product of wine-making. Grape pips are washed, dried, ground and pressed with the aid of heat, then further refined to produce oil with a light texture that is virtually odour-free.

Therapeutic use

Grapeseed oil is high in linoleic acid. It is non-greasy and suits all skin and hair types. It is difficult to obtain an unrefined version (which has a very unpleasant smell), so it

Grapeseed oil comes from the pips of the grape

should ideally be mixed with other, less refined oils to boost its nutrient content. It costs less than most other carrier oils and allergic reactions are extremely rare.

Hazelnut (Corylus avallana)
Description
This oil is derived from hazelnuts, which grow on tall shrubs found in the wild throughout Europe. Hazelnuts are quite low in fat and contain useful levels of Vitamin E. The oil is more often used in food than skincare and makes a delicious addition to salad dressings.

Therapeutic use
Hazelnut oil is slightly astringent, making it useful for oily or combination skins. It has a short shelf-life and is best stored in the fridge. Avoid in cases of nut allergy.

Hazelnut oil suits oily skin as it is slightly astringent

Jojoba (Simmondsia chinensis)
Description
Jojoba is a liquid, golden-coloured wax, rather than an oil. It derives from small, dark-brown beans found on a woody evergreen shrub with flat green leathery leaves that grows in the deserts of Southern Arizona, Southern California, Mexico and Argentina. It can survive without rain for many weeks at high temperatures and is nicknamed 'desert gold'.

Therapeutic use
Jojoba has been prized for centuries for skin and hair care and is now widely used commercially. It offers some protection from UV rays and features in many sunscreen products. It is light, highly penetrative and high in fatty acids and Vitamin E. Its waxy substance is chemically similar to sebum and it lubricates and softens the skin, acting as a medium for holding in moisture and regulating the flow of sebum. Its ability to normalise the production of sebum makes it suitable for all skin types and for softening and conditioning hair. It is useful for treating psoriasis and eczema, and for controlling dandruff. It is one of the more expensive oils and can be blended to enrich other, cheaper oils.

Jojoba oil suits all skin types

Olive oil (Olea europea)
Description
Most olive oil comes from Spain, Italy and Greece where the soil and warm temperatures are ideal for growth. Although it can take up to ten years for an olive tree to bear fruit, it can live for over 600 years. Olive oil is widely used in cooking and is regarded as effective in combating high cholesterol levels, due to its monounsaturated fatty acids. Several grades of olive oil are available; extra-virgin olive oil is

considered superior as it is obtained from the first pressing of the olives.

Therapeutic use

This oil was the first to be used in beauty treatments by ancient Egyptians, who saw it as a gift from their goddess Isis. Olive oil is excellent for chapped, scaly skin conditions such as eczema. It also relieves sore, tense muscles and reduces swelling. Its warming effects make it suitable for winter use. When applied to the scalp, it can make the hair shafts less prone to splitting and gives body and shine to coarse thick hair. A few drops applied to the ends of very dry hair will tame flyaway ends. Because of its viscous consistency and strong aroma, which does not appeal to everyone, it is best mixed (up to 50 per cent) with a lighter oil.

Olive oil is excellent for chapped, scaly skin conditions

Ayurvedic blends

It is common in India for a blend of oils and herbs to be used in head massage and these blends are becoming increasingly popular outside India. Descriptions of some of the herbs used in blends follow.

Amla

This herb is little known in the West but used extensively in Indian communities throughout the world. Amla is extracted from Indian Gooseberry, which is high in Vitamin C. It feeds and nourishes the scalp and strengthens hair roots.

Brahmi

Extracted from Indian Pennyworth, brahmi helps to control stress-related problems as it has a calming effect on the nerves. It also provides relief from dandruff.

Bringraj

This Ayurvedic herb is found throughout India and southwestern USA and its name means 'ruler of the hair'. Its oil deters greying, darkens the hair, slows down hair loss, relieves headaches and promotes deep sleep.

Henna

Henna (mendi oil) is non-toxic and popular as a natural conditioner for all hair types. Different types of henna are available. Some condition the hair without colouring, making it lustrous and shiny.

Shikakai

This comes from the crushed pods of Acacia Concinna, a small shrub found mainly in South Asia. The pods are ground into a powder, mixed with water and used to wash and condition the hair. It has antiseptic properties and is a popular remedy for dandruff, eczema and dry scalp conditions.

For suppliers of Ayurvedic blends see 'Useful products'.

casestudy

Lesley reports on how oils have benefited her hair:

'My hair is fine and straight and I have it highlighted regularly. It is prone to be dry, flat and flyaway and can look dull and lifeless, even after using commercial conditioners. My Indian Head Massage training was a lifeline for my hair as it introduced me to the benefits of using oils. I use an Ayurvedic blend containing coconut oil, henna, amla and lemon – it has a fantastic aroma. I warm the oil and massage it well into my scalp, run it through the ends and leave it for on for an hour, or sometimes overnight. After use my hair looks thicker, bouncy, shiny and smooth and feels fabulous to touch. I thoroughly recommend using oils to promote healthy hair.'

Applying oils to the scalp

'Shiro Abhyanga' is the name given to Ayurvedic head massage and includes the application of oils according to constitutional type as well as working on marma points of the head.

Oils like sesame, almond and olive are beneficial for treating the hyperactivity and dryness of excess vata. Spicy oils such as mustard are heating in nature and help balance kapha; sesame oil is also beneficial in small amounts. Oils that are cooling in nature, such as coconut, balance excess pitta.

Oil is normally applied to three spots on the head and then spread over the scalp using various massage strokes.

First spot on scalp where oil is applied

1 The fontanelle (adhipati marma – the soft spot on an infant's head), located eight finger-widths (of person being treated) above the third-eye, is the first spot. This is a most important marma point, governing prana of the entire body. Oil is poured here while making small circular movements with fingertips of the other hand.

2 The circular area on the crown is the second spot. A most important nadi (energy channel) called 'sushumna' which originates in the first chakra terminates

Second spot on scalp where oil is applied

here. Even Hindus who shave their heads don't shave this area but twist and knot the hairs to stimulate fine capillaries in the roots and improve the flow of prana.

45

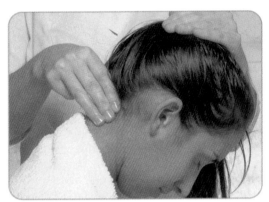
Third spot on scalp where oil is applied

3 The third spot is where the neck meets the skull, either side of the last two palpable vertebrae, between two important marmas called 'krikatika'. With the head forward, oil is applied here using small circular movements.

Once the oil has been applied, 'shampoo' the scalp thoroughly and then apply a range of scalp massage movements of your (or your client's) choice. (See also Chapter 6 for an explanation of the terms and a detailed routine.) Use tabla, light hacking or champi to

stimulate the circulatory and nervous systems. Take the head between your palms and apply pressure all around. Finish by laying your hands lightly on top of the head, taking three deep breaths and sweeping down the sides of the head.

- ॐ Remember to use a towel around the shoulders to avoid staining clothing
- ॐ Start with a teaspoon of oil on each spot – you may need a little more if the hair is long and very thick.
- ॐ Leave oil on for a couple of hours or overnight if possible – place a towel over the pillow to avoid staining.
- ॐ To remove oil easily, massage a small amount of shampoo through the hair before adding water. This emulsifies the oil, which then washes out with ease.
- ॐ You can provide oil for clients to use at home.

You can also massage your own scalp using oils to suit your skin type. Apply the oil as above and massage thoroughly, using your favourite Indian Head Massage strokes.

FAQs

What is Shirodhara?

This is an ancient Ayurvedic practice in which warmed sesame oil (often infused with herbs) is gently poured over the forehead as the client lies on a special massage couch which allows the oil to drain away. It often follows a seated head massage and is used to calm the nervous system and the mind. 'Shiro' means 'head' and 'dhara' means 'the dripping of oil like a thread'.

I think my clients would prefer a massage with oil to a dry massage. Can I do an Indian Head Massage treatment using oil all the way through?

The techniques in an Indian Head Massage treatment (described in Chapter 6) are designed to be performed as a dry massage to achieve maximum therapeutic benefits. If oil is used, the hands tend to slide over the scalp so it is not possible to adequately relieve tight muscles. It is more beneficial to do a short massage with oil at the end of a treatment.

Which essential oils are recommended for a hair oil blend?

Qualified aromatherapists use a range of essential oils on the scalp. These are diluted in carrier oil and include rosemary, sandalwood, geranium, eucalyptus, tea tree and lemon. Rosemary is used to stimulate hair growth. Sandalwood soothes the skin and has powerful germicidal and antiseptic properties. Geranium, eucalyptus and tea tree help to combat head lice. Lemon is cleansing, anti-microbial and controls the flow of sebum. Jasmine oil is popular in India for its beautiful scent and is good in tiny amounts for skin that is hot, dry and sensitive.

What can be used to condition the hair if a client does not like oil?

Aloe vera gel offers an alternative to oil and is excellent for skin and hair care. It is rich in vitamins and minerals, and has anti-bacterial and anti-fungal properties making it useful for conditions such as dandruff. It has superior anti-inflammatory properties and is used to soothe dry, itching skin. It aids cell regeneration, stimulates hair growth and offers some protection from UV rays. It can be mixed with jojoba, making an excellent cream for application to the scalp and skin.

contra-indications and cautions

Contraindications are signs or symptoms indicating that a treatment should not be carried out or that certain areas should be avoided. Signs are things that we may notice about someone (such as hair loss) whereas symptoms are things that a person complains of or will report if appropriate questions are put to them. If you are a massage therapist, contraindications should be checked thoroughly in the initial consultation and re-checked each time a person comes in again for treatment.

From a safety viewpoint, if a person presents with a contagious disorder, it can be passed on to the therapist and others and the condition may be worsened by treatment. Similarly, any therapist suffering from a contagious disorder should not carry out treatments until the condition has been treated and cleared. From a comfort viewpoint, if someone is experiencing pain, they may be unable to relax and enjoy the benefits of the treatment. Most importantly, if anyone suffers harm due to your negligence, it reflects badly on your professionalism and may lead to legal action being taken against you.

Levels of contraindication

The list of contraindications for Indian Head Massage (or indeed any form of massage) is not completely fixed, although some therapists wish that it were! Some reasons not to treat are very obvious, but others will depend on factors such as the severity of the condition, the size of area affected and sometimes the age of the person being treated. If you are a qualified therapist, the knowledge you acquire through your training and experience, as well as common sense and the guidelines of any professional organisations to which you belong, should help you to choose the appropriate course of action.

Some contraindications are total, meaning that treatment should not be carried out until the condition has completely cleared. These include serious illnesses; infectious diseases passed around in the air through coughs and sneezes; and contagious diseases passed by direct contact, such as touching the infected area. Others are local contraindications, meaning that treatment may be carried out but certain areas should be avoided.

Other presenting conditions may be treated following advice from the individual's medical practitioner. This advice can be sought in writing by the therapist, or verbally by the client, who should sign a form to state that advice was obtained. If medical advice cannot be obtained, clients must indemnify their condition in writing prior to treatment (i.e. specify the condition, and agree that all aspects of the treatment have been fully explained and that they agree to have the treatment). However, it is important that a therapist knows when treatment should definitely not be given and that they do not treat in this case, even if the person wishes the treatment to go ahead. When liaising with medical practitioners, be aware that another practitioner's insurance may not cover them to give consent to complementary therapy treatments. Therapists should make it clear that they are seeking advice about the suitability of the proposed treatment and should include literature on Indian Head Massage, including its methodology, benefits, contraindications and effects. A doctor cannot be expected to give advice about a treatment of which they have no knowledge. If a client who comes to you for massage is already being treated by a medical doctor or another practitioner for a particular condition, you should refer to them before treating the client.

Some conditions can be treated, but may require additional caution during treatment.

The contraindications and precautions for Indian Head Massage are outlined in this section. They should be included in a confidential pre-treatment questionnaire, which you should give to all clients to complete before their first treatment. You will find a sample questionnaire on page 51.

Total contraindications

Treatment should not be carried out until these conditions are completely cleared.

High temperature or fever

This is usually caused by a viral or bacterial infection and is thought to be the body's natural defence mechanism as it tries to reach a temperature in which the virus or bacteria cannot survive. Fever can also be a symptom of certain blood disorders, respiratory problems, psychological or emotional disorders, as well as dehydration, teething, and the after-effects of immunisations. These can trigger the immune system to produce chemicals that affect the normal functioning of the hypothalamus, the heat-regulating centre in the brain.

When fever is present, the circulation is already over-stimulated as the body works hard to combat infection, so it should not be further stimulated by massage.

Infectious diseases

If someone presents with an infectious or contagious disease they should not be treated because of the risk of spreading the infection. Examples are heavy colds, flu, tuberculosis, chicken pox, measles and mumps.

Skin or scalp infections

Contagious conditions on the skin and scalp should be avoided because of the risk of cross-infection. These include:

- infestations such as pediculosis capitis (head lice) and scabies (tiny itch mite)
- fungal infections such as ringworm of the body (tinea corporis) or ringworm of the scalp (tinea capitis)

CLIENT CONSULTATION FORM – INDIAN HEAD MASSAGE

This information is strictly confidential and will not be shared with a third party without your written consent

Name: _____ Date: _____

Address: _____ Client No. _____

_____ Referred by: _____

_____ Tel: _____

Mobile: _____ Email: _____

D.O.B. _____

Conditions	
Hair type – normal, dry, oily, fine, brittle (circle)	
Hair loss	
Premature greying	
Dandruff	
Headaches/migraines	
Stiffness in neck/shoulders	
Psoriasis/eczema	
TMJ problems	
Tinnitus	
Eyestrain	
Sinus problems	
Sleeping problems	
Anxiety / Stress	
Depression	
Other (please specify)	

Lifestyle	
Daily water consumption?	
Do you smoke? If so, how much?	
Daily tea/coffee consumption?	
Healthy diet?	
Weekly alcohol consumption?	
Do you take regular exercise?	
Do you see daylight in workplace?	
How are your stress levels on a scale of 1(low) –10 (high)?	
Causes of stress?	
Any other issues?	

Contraindications   (total /local) CIRCLE OR TICK
Infection/disease/fever
Under influence of alcohol or drugs
Diarrhoea or vomiting
Head lice
Folliculitis (sycosis barbae)
Conjunctivitis
Skin or scalp diseases
Undiagnosed lumps and bumps
Localised swelling or inflammation
Cuts/bruises/abrasions
Sunburnt skin
Scar tissue (how old?)
Recent fractures (how old?)
Hormonal implants (area to be avoided)
Cervical spondylitis
After a heavy meal

Medical clearance + Precautions CIRCLE OR TICK
Cardiovascular conditions
Hemophilia
Medical oedema
Osteoporosis/arthritis/acute rheumatism
Nervous/psychotic conditions
Epilepsy
Recent operations (how long ago and reason?)
Diabetes
Asthma
Nervous system dysfunctions
Trapped/inflamed nerve
Postural deformities/spastic conditions
Whiplash/slipped disc
Undiagnosed pain
M.E.
First trimester of pregnancy
On prescribed medication (explain below)
Already being treated by GP or other therapist

Notes: (use this box to comment on GP referrals, any presenting conditions, lifestyle issues or contraindications circled or ticked above. Continue on a separate sheet if necessary. Each treatment should then be recorded, including the date, how the client felt before, during and after the treatment and details of any homecare advice given.)

Client's signature:_____ Date:_____

Therapist's signature:_____ Date:_____

Sample pre–treatment questionnaire

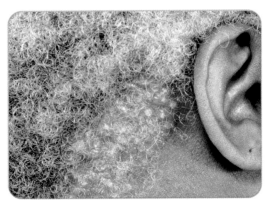
Scalp ringworm (tinea capitis)

☞ bacterial infections such as impetigo, conjunctivitis (inflammation of lining of eyelid and mucus membrane covering the eye, which can be due to bacteria or a virus), folliculitis (bacterial inflammation of the hair follicles and surrounding skin, which sometimes affects men in the beard area, where it is termed 'barber's itch' or 'sycosis barbae')

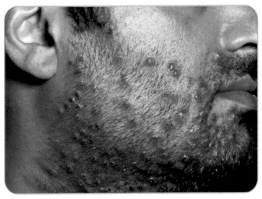
Sycosis barbae

☞ viral infections such as herpes zoster (shingles).

People under the influence of recreational drugs or alcohol

This can inhibit or distort response to treatment and may result in the person becoming aggressive or over-emotional. It can also make them feel dizzy or nauseous due to increased blood flow to the head.

Diarrhoea and vomiting

The person will not feel like (nor will they benefit from) having treatment in this case. If they do not already know the cause, they should be advised to seek it.

Local contraindications

In these cases, treatment may be carried out, but certain areas should be avoided.

Skin diseases

Avoid areas affected by herpes simplex (cold sores) or boils. Weeping eczema can be infected so should be avoided, as should any inflamed area of eczema or psoriasis. Where psoriasis or eczema is not sore, light massage is beneficial as it aids the removal of dead skin cells – the flaking skin may look unsightly but is not harmful to the therapist.

A cold sore (herpes simplex)

Undiagnosed problem areas

In the case of undiagnosed lumps, bumps, areas of pain, localised swelling or inflammation, avoid massage over the area and refer the person to their medical practitioner for a diagnosis if the cause is unknown.

Cuts, bruises, abrasions, sunburn

The area will be sore to touch and pressure from massage may cause further pain and damage.

Scar tissue following recent injury or operation

Do not massage until the tissue has fully healed and can withstand pressure. After that, massage is very beneficial in breaking down adhesions. Some guidelines suggest that scar tissue following a major operation should be avoided for around two years and that small scars should be avoided for six months. Massage can prevent the formation of scar tissue and in many cases can be done sooner, depending on the speed of the healing process.

Recent fractures

Allow the area to heal before applying pressure. As a guideline, allow at least three months before working on the area.

Hormonal implants

This is a form of female contraception using progestin, a synthetic form of the female hormone progesterone. Tiny, rod-like implants containing the medication are inserted by a health professional under the skin of a woman's upper arm. They release progestin

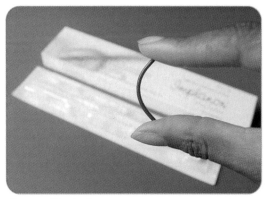

Hormonal implants

for up to seven years, depending on the type of implant. Do not massage directly over the area.

Cervical spondylitis

This is a form of arthritis in the neck due to thinning of the discs, causing the spaces between the vertebrae to become narrower and growth of bone spurs (osteophytes) at the edges of the vertebra and facet joints. It is associated with the ageing process. Bulging discs or osteophytes can pinch nerve roots (causing pain or numbness in the arm) or pinch the vertebral artery (reducing blood supply to part of the brain that controls balance, leading to dizziness).

After a heavy meal

After a meal, blood is diverted to the digestive system to help with digestion of food. Massage immediately after a heavy meal is best avoided, as it will divert blood away from the digestive system and hinder the absorption of nutrients.

Medical clearance or specialist permission

Depending on the severity of the condition, medical clearance may be necessary for some individuals. Once medical clearance has been obtained, the therapist should proceed with caution, particularly if it is the first time they are treating the person. Depending on their state, it may be necessary to offer a shorter treatment, use lighter pressure or avoid certain areas. Reactions should be monitored carefully.

The following conditions may require medical clearance before Indian Head Massage.

Serious cardiovascular conditions

These include thrombosis, phlebitis, hypertension, hypotension, and heart conditions.

Anyone suffering from phlebitis (inflammation of a vein) or thrombosis (formation of blood clots in blood vessels) is at risk of an embolism (a blood clot that becomes detached and carried to another part of body).

People with very high blood pressure (hypertension) are susceptible to blood clot formation and drugs taken to lower blood pressure can make a person light-headed and dizzy after treatment – monitor reactions carefully. Since massage is said to lower blood pressure, those under medical supervision for hypertension should ensure their practitioner is aware they are having treatments so that medication can be monitored and altered if necessary. Advice regarding any alterations in medication should only be given by the medical practitioner.

Many people have naturally low blood pressure (hypotension) which causes no problems, so long as it is stable. However, since massage can lower blood pressure, a person with hypotension may feel light-headed or dizzy after treatment, so allow them extra time to relax before standing up. In some cases a more vigorous massage can help prevent this. If a client with low blood pressure is prone to fainting, treatment is not recommended.

Haemophilia

This is a hereditary disorder in which the blood clots slowly due to a deficiency of coagulation factors. The condition is almost exclusively restricted to males but females can carry the disorder without any effects. Deep pressure from massage could cause internal haemorrhage.

Medical oedema

Oedema is swelling due to retention of fluid in the tissues. It is important to know the cause of oedema as it can be due to a serious medical condition, such as heart or kidney failure, cirrhosis of the liver or acute nephritis (kidney disease). It can also be the result of an allergy or taking certain drugs. If oedema is simply due to a sluggish lymphatic system, massage is very beneficial.

Osteoporosis

This condition is characterised by a decrease in bone mass and density, causing bones to become brittle and fragile. If severe, medical advice may be required before treatment as deep pressure may cause fractures.

Arthritis

Inflammation of a joint (or joints) causing pain, swelling and stiffness. When clients present with arthritis it may require medical advice or it may be a local contraindication, depending on the location and severity of the condition.

Acute rheumatism

Rheumatism is defined as any painful disorder of the joints, muscles or connective tissues. Rheumatoid arthritis is a chronic auto-immune disease with inflammation of the joints and marked deformities. Medical clearance may be required, depending on the area affected and severity of the condition.

Nervous/psychotic conditions

It is advisable to seek medical advice, as deep relaxation caused by massage may trigger emotional problems in the client that a therapist may not be qualified to deal with.

Epilepsy

Epilepsy is a disorder of the brain that results in recurrent, unprovoked seizures. There are various forms of epilepsy, from mild to severe (petit mal to grand mal). Medical advice is recommended due to the complexity of this condition and the risk that deep relaxation or over-stimulation could provoke a convulsion. If using oils, be aware that some smells can trigger epilepsy.

Recent operations

Depending on the site of surgery, it may be a total contraindication or it may be necessary to get medical clearance before treatment.

Diabetes

Diabetics are prone to arteriosclerosis (hardening of the arteries), high blood pressure, dry or damaged skin with poor healing qualities, poor circulation and oedema. Diabetes causes the capillaries to thicken, which reduces blood supply to nerves – monitor pressure carefully as clients may have a loss in sensory functioning and be unable to give accurate feedback. Massage can lower blood sugar levels so a person who is diabetic may need something sweet (e.g. fruit juice) following a treatment.

Asthma

If attacks are frequent or severe, specialist permission should be sought. Massage of the upper back can help between attacks but should not be used during an attack.

Cancer

When treating someone who is undergoing treatment for cancer you should have approval from their medical practitioner. Nowadays, massage is successfully used alongside cancer care as it can help the person deal with the emotional stress of the condition as well as minimise some of the side effects of the treatment. It is important to know as much as possible about the type of cancer involved and the effects of treatment. Some hospices and cancer resource centres offer training for massage therapists.

Whiplash/head or neck injuries/ slipped disc

Seek medical clearance as massage may worsen the condition; with old injuries, massage can reduce scar tissue, decrease pain and increase mobility.

Undiagnosed pain

Pain is a signal of a problem somewhere in the body and although massage can help relieve pain by releasing endorphins (the body's own natural morphine) the person should be advised to seek a medical diagnosis if pain is severe and the cause unknown.

Dysfunctions of the nervous system

Therapists should ensure that they gather as much information as possible about the particular condition. Although massage can ease stress and help to maintain mobility, over–stimulation may cause muscle spasm. In some cases, a shorter treatment may be more beneficial. The comfort of the client during treatment should be carefully considered. Conditions that therapists may encounter include the following.

Multiple sclerosis

This is a disorder of the central nervous system marked by weakness, numbness, loss of muscle co-ordination, and problems with vision, speech, and bladder control. Multiple sclerosis is thought to be an auto-immune disease, in which the body's immune system destroys myelin, a substance that insulates nerve fibres, speeding up transmission of nerve signals.

Cerebral palsy

This is a non-progressive disorder of move-ment resulting from damage to the brain before, during or immediately after birth. The most common condition is a spastic paralysis, leading to lack of balance and contracture of the limbs. Hearing and vision may also be affected.

Parkinson's disease

This is a progressive disease, characterised by death of nerve cells in a specific area of the brain called the basal ganglia. Parkinson patients lack the neurotransmitter dopamine and have symptoms such as tremors, speech impediments, movement difficulties and often dementia later in the course of the disease.

Motor neurone disease

This is a chronic, slowly progressive disease of motor nerves, causing muscle wasting, weakness and paralysis.

Bell's palsy

Paralysis of the facial nerve (the fifth cranial nerve), usually affecting muscles on one side of the face. It can occur as a consequence of MS, a viral infection, or other infections. It has an acute onset and can be transient or permanent, although most cases make a complete recovery. Facial massage and facial exercises help muscles regain their tone.

Inflamed, trapped or pinched nerve

Avoid massage over the area as it may worsen the inflammation and cause pain. Refer to medical practitioner if the condition is undiagnosed or severe. Loss of sensation due to a trapped nerve may inhibit or distort client's response to pressure, discomfort and pain. However, release of tension in muscles through massage may reduce pressure on trapped or pinched nerves.

Medication

Medication may distort a client's feedback regarding pressure, discomfort and pain.

Depending on the medication and its effects, medical clearance may be necessary before treatment where clients are taking the following drugs:

- anticoagulants, such as Warfarin and Heparin, prescribed to thin the blood (deep massage could cause bruising or internal bleeding)
- steroids long term (can cause thinning of the skin, osteoporosis and capillary damage)
- cytoxic drugs (for treatment of cancer), which cause a reduction of blood-clotting 'platelets' (subsequently, heavy massage may cause bleeding under the skin).

Cautions

Extra caution may be required when treating clients with the following conditions.

Elderly, very young or very nervous clients

A shorter treatment may be more appropriate. You should explain the procedure fully and check that they are not having treatment because someone else thinks it a good idea. Ensure that they are warm and comfortable throughout the treatment.

Myalgic encephalomyelitis (ME)

Clients with ME (also known as chronic fatigue syndrome) can benefit from Indian Head Massage, which may reduce anxiety about their condition. It is advisable to avoid deep pressure on tender areas. A shorter and more relaxing treatment is recommended, as ME sufferers often find a full or stimulating treatment exhausting.

casestudy

James talks here about an experience as a practitioner:

'I am qualified in Indian Head Massage and had been practising for two years, mainly in offices. I went on a meditation weekend and one of the other participants, John, aged 29, had ME. When he heard I was a massage therapist he requested a treatment. I had not worked on anyone with ME before. John was thin, pale and low in energy. I was aware of the advice to work lightly on those with ME but I thought it was over-cautious, and felt sure my regular massage would energise him, as it did my other clients. I did my normal massage on him at 7.30 in the evening. By 8 he was in bed and was not seen again until 9 the next morning. I was very alarmed by this. His body could not take the stimulating treatment and it had exhausted him. It really taught me a lesson and I now adhere to advice on contraindications and precautions, and have since worked successfully on clients with ME.'

Postural defects

Postural defects include kyphosis, scoliosis and lordosis. Ensure that the client is comfortable during treatment: extra support may be needed for neck or lower back. Shorter treatments may be necessary.

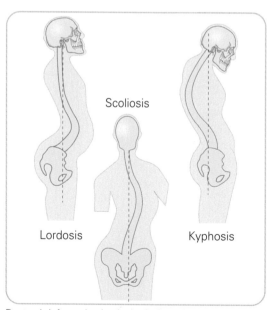

Postural defects: kyphosis, lordosis and scoliosis

Scoliosis

Lordosis

Kyphosis

Very large or very small-framed clients, disabled clients

Ensure that the chair is comfortable and check that the pressure applied is appropriate. Indian Head Massage can easily be carried out on someone who is in a wheelchair. As always, approach each case individually.

Allergies

Patch tests may be required if using oils on sensitive individuals.

Pregnancy

There is no need for an established pregnancy (after twelve weeks) to be a contraindication unless there are serious complications. Care should be taken to ensure the client is comfortable. The therapist should be aware that some pregnant women experience dizziness and high blood pressure. Avoid treatment in the first three months, particularly with a history of miscarriage.

FAQs

Why should massage be avoided in the first three months of pregnancy?

During the first twelve weeks, hormone levels are rapidly changing in order to stabilise the pregnancy and the foetus is not fully implanted in the uterus until at least the eighth week. The first eight weeks of pregnancy (embryonic period) is a period of rapid development, when all body systems are being established. More growth and development happens at this time that at any other period in our lifetime. Although Indian Head Massage is highly unlikely to cause miscarriage, miscarriages most commonly occur during the first twelve weeks, and the client may associate the two events. It is best to let the body stabilise until the first twelve weeks are over and the mother knows that there are no problems with the pregnancy. After that, massage can be very beneficial.

My partner is completely bald. Can I still give him a head massage?

Baldness is not a contraindication, and although you will be unable to carry out techniques involving the hair, such as hair tugging, all other techniques can be carried out, including those on the scalp.

What is a treatment plan?

A treatment plan is a strategy for dealing with a client's particular condition in the best possible way. It is formulated following the consultation in conjunction with the client. For example, if someone suffers from insomnia, it may be best for treatments to be scheduled in the evening to promote sleep, or if someone has specific areas of tension, you may need to spend more time working on those areas. Specific scalp conditions may require certain oils to be used and extra support may be needed for some clients (e.g. a cushion to support the lower back in cases of lordosis). All of these points should be included on the treatment plan, which should be reviewed each time the client comes for treatment to see if any changes are needed.

I am a student of Indian Head Massage and would like my father, who has Parkinson's disease, to be one of my case studies. Would this be okay?

If you need to seek medical advice before treating a client (as in cases of Parkinson's disease), it is recommended that you wait until you are qualified. This is a sensible precaution that protects everyone involved.

an indian head massage treatment

Massage techniques

Indian Head Massage techniques consist of variations of classical massage movements and some that are specific to Indian Head Massage. Treatment is traditionally done through the clothing, the use of oil being optional. In India, massage skills are passed down through generations and it is quite common to find variations from one family or region to the next. The main techniques employed in a treatment are described next.

Effleurage

From the French 'effleurer' meaning 'to touch lightly', this is a gentle, sweeping, relaxing stroke, with varying levels of pressure. It is used at the beginning and end of a massage, to soothe, relax and improve circulation. It prepares the body for massage, introduces the client to the therapist's touch, links movements and warms the area. It can also be used with firm pressure once muscles have been relaxed, to help eliminate toxins.

Petrissage (Kneading)

From the French 'petrir' meaning 'to knead' or rub with force, this stroke uses both kneading and rubbing movements to manipulate tissues and muscles. It uses pressure of the hands (or the fingers, thumbs or knuckles) to stretch and knead tissues and break down tension and stiffness caused by a build-up of toxins such as lactic acid. Although a firm stroke, it is generally more relaxing than invigorating because it releases tightness and toxins. It should not be used on bony or delicate areas.

Compression

This is a form of petrissage in which muscles are gently pressed against a surface (such as the upper arms or scalp) with both hands and slowly released. It increases blood flow and relieves muscular tension and pain.

Friction

From the Latin 'fricare', meaning to rub down, friction techniques use the whole hand or just the fingers, thumb, or palm to compress tissue against bone, rather than sliding over the skin. Friction is often used for work on a small area or specific areas of tightness. It improves circulation, generates local heat, releases muscular tension and encourages hair growth when done on the scalp.

Percussion

From the Latin 'percutere', meaning 'to hit', percussion techniques are brisk, invigorating and stimulating. The hands are used to strike the body rapidly and suddenly. It stimulates the nerves, improves circulation, energises mind and body and improves muscle tone. The form of percussion used in Indian Head Massage is tapotement, which uses light, brisk movements. The movements include hacking (with the sides of the little fingers); champi (hands joined); cupping (using cupped hands) and tabla (drumming with fingers).

Pressure points

This is the application of pressure on specific points, such as marma and sinus points, using fingers or thumbs to release blocked energy, improve circulation and stimulate the nerves. This technique can also relieve sinus congestion, encourage lymph drainage and restore energy balance to the body.

Vibrations

Vibrations are shaking or oscillating movements that use one or both hands and either the whole palms or the fingertips. The palms or fingertips are placed on the muscle and while retaining firm, deep contact, briskly moved up and down or side to side. This is used when muscles are extremely tight and not responding to petrissage or friction. Vibrations help release pain and tension and clear nerve pathways. Although not used in classical Indian Head Massage, this technique can benefit very tight shoulders.

Passive joint movements

Passive movements require the client to relax and let the therapist gently take a joint through its natural range of movement. This improves mobility and releases tension (e.g. around the shoulder joint).

Specialised Indian Head Massage techniques

Champissage/Champi

From the Hindi word 'champi' meaning 'head massage' (from which the word 'shampoo' is derived), this tapotement movement is similar to hacking but the hands are placed together as if in prayer. With elbows extended and loose wrists, the back and shoulders are struck with the little finger side (ulnar side) of the hands. It warms and invigorates the receiver, increases blood circulation and tones muscles.

Tabla

This tapotement movement is used on the scalp and involves gently tapping with fingers as if playing the piano or tabla drum. It energises and stimulates the nervous system.

Hair tugging

This involves gripping the hair at its base and moving the scalp underneath while keeping close contact with the scalp. It improves blood circulation to the hair follicles. Care must be taken not to pull too hard.

Plucking

This stimulating movement involves making a loose, claw shape with the hands, spreading fingers wide, gently placing them on the head and briskly bringing them together as they come off the scalp.

'Shampooing'

As if washing the hair, fingers and thumbs are spread over the scalp, making small circular movements to 'shampoo' with medium pressure. Thumbs can be used around the occipital area. It releases tension in scalp muscles and stimulates circulation to hair follicles.

Holding and stroking

These are relaxing techniques done on the head and face to calm and soothe the nervous system.

Personal preparation

Always ensure that you are adequately prepared to give a treatment. Do not treat someone if you are extremely tired or mentally low. If you are a professional therapist, remember that you don't have a second chance to make a first impression, so your appearance and that of your workplace is paramount. The following points are very important.

- Clothing should be clean, smart and easy to work in. Shoes should be comfortable for standing, as you will be on your feet.
- You will be working in close proximity to clients, so ensure good personal hygiene (daily showering, clean teeth and fresh breath).
- Hands should be clean and the nails short. Any cuts or abrasions should be covered.
- Watches and jewellery should be removed.
- Long hair should be tied back.
- Avoid wearing strong perfumes, which can be distracting and may cause headaches.

Check your posture and keep your weight evenly distributed on outer edges of your feet as good posture will prevent aches and pains and enable you to work longer without becoming too tired. Relax your face muscles and smile as you work! Relax your shoulders and remember to bend your knees when working from the side to keep your back upright. (See Chapter 7 for more on self-care.)

Treatment preparation

It is important to be well prepared and have everything you need within reach before beginning a treatment. This will ensure that the client can relax and enjoy its benefits. Use a quiet room where you will not be interrupted and check that heating, lighting and ventilation are conducive to relaxation. Some people like to have soft music playing, while others prefer silence, so check the preference of each client.

You will need the following items:

- a consultation form (see the example on page 51)
- a comfortable, upright, low-backed chair that allows access to the upper back
- a cushion to make the chair more comfortable and allow for height adjustment
- a small cushion or rolled-up towel to support the head when doing face massage
- hair elastic, hair clips or headband to keep long hair away from face, neck and shoulders for the first part of the treatment
- a small container for the client's jewellery, which should be removed before treatment
- a towel to cover shoulders if using oils
- a selection of oils for scalp massage
- water and glass for refreshment after treatment.

Before you begin

- Explain the treatment and what it entails.
- Check for contraindications (see Chapter 5). If you are a professional therapist, this will form part of your consultation.

61

Note – If the client is less than 16 years old, a parent or guardian must be present and give written consent.

🔾 Ask client to remove heavy garments such as sweaters and jewellery such as necklace, earrings or hair accessories and put them in a container.

🔾 Tidy long hair out of the way.

🔾 Some clients feel more comfortable and grounded if they remove their shoes. Ensure they are sitting comfortably with arms and legs uncrossed and provide support under feet if necessary.

🔾 Wash your hands and begin the treatment.

Indian Head Massage routine

Here is our suggestion for a treatment taking about 30 minutes. If you perform an oil massage at the end, the treatment can be extended to 40 minutes. Our treatment begins by grounding, then working on the face, shoulders, arms, neck and scalp, followed by chakra energy balancing and oil massage of the scalp (optional). You can choose to vary this routine appropriately, as you wish.

Grounding

Standing behind client with your feet hip-width apart, place a small cushion or rolled-up towel behind the neck to support the head and lay your hands lightly on top of the shoulders. Ask the client to take three deep breaths through the nose and breathe deeply along with them. This calms and relaxes both of you before treatment begins.

The face massage

Starting on the face tends to make the client relax quickly. It also means that you don't break the flow by stopping to clean your hands before moving from scalp to face.

1 Effleurage

With your fingertips, effleurage the face, working from the mid-line towards the ears. Work up from the chin to the forehead.

Effleurage

2 Frontal pressure points

Using pads of your middle fingers (or ring fingers for lighter pressure), press nine points on the forehead, holding each for five seconds.

1 Point 1 is between eyebrows (the staphani marma).

2 Point 2 is in the middle of eyebrows (the avarta marma).

3 Point 3 is on the temples (the shanka marma).

4 Work on three points from the middle of the forehead to the sides (points 4, 5 and 6).

5 Then work along the hairline in three places, working outwards (points 7, 8 and 9).

6 Finally, sweep with your fingers from points 7, 4 and 1 out to sides.

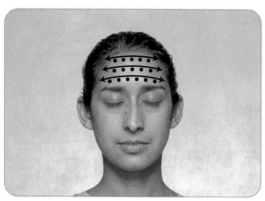
Frontal pressure points

3 Pressure points – eyes

Apply pressure for 2–3 seconds on points all around the eye sockets, moving out along the top and inwards underneath. Don't slide the fingers along. Instead, lift them when moving from one point to the next. You will work on the avarta marma (midpoint above the eyes) and apanga marma (outer corners of eyes).

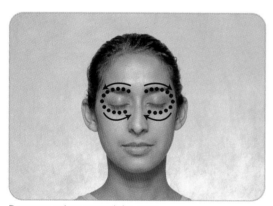
Pressure points around the eyes

4 Pressure points – nose and cheeks

Apply pressure for two or three seconds on points along sides of the nose working down to the nostrils (phana marma) and follow the curve under the cheekbones (shringataka

marma) to a point in front of the ears (feel for a small depression on the TMJ – this is an important acupressure point for many ear disorders). For sinus problems, apply friction along sides of the nose to the nostrils and then on the cheeks (maxillary sinuses).

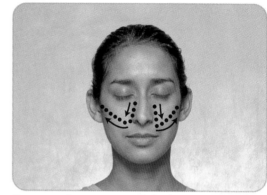
Pressure points on nose and cheeks

5 Jawline

With your thumbs on the chin and index fingers underneath, apply pressure and release; repeat at 1cm intervals working out towards the ears. Apply friction in small circles along same area before stroking out to the ears three times.

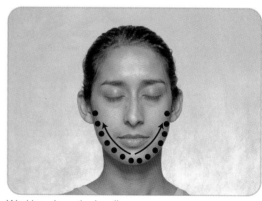
Working along the jaw line

6 Friction (jaw)

Apply friction with medium pressure at temporomandibular joint and masseter muscles before stroking down towards the neck.

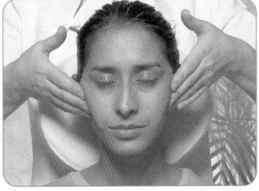

Friction on masseter muscles

7 Ears

Starting at the ear lobes, work up and down the ears using your thumb and forefinger. Squeeze and release, apply friction and gently pull ears as you work up and down three times. The ears are rich in acupressure points, so take your time on this part of the massage.

8 Friction (temples)

Using your fingers or the heels of your hands, apply gentle circular friction on temples (the shanka marma) making six full circles. This helps to direct energy to the brain and mind and is excellent for eyestrain and tension headaches. Make six circles further back on the utkshepa marma to calm the mind and control excess vata.

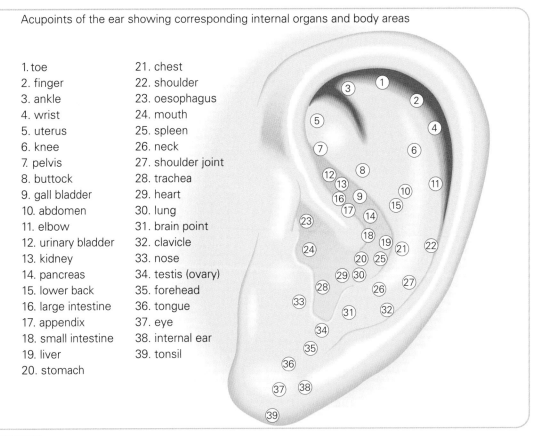

Acupoints of the ear showing corresponding internal organs and body areas

1. toe
2. finger
3. ankle
4. wrist
5. uterus
6. knee
7. pelvis
8. buttock
9. gall bladder
10. abdomen
11. elbow
12. urinary bladder
13. kidney
14. pancreas
15. lower back
16. large intestine
17. appendix
18. small intestine
19. liver
20. stomach

21. chest
22. shoulder
23. oesophagus
24. mouth
25. spleen
26. neck
27. shoulder joint
28. trachea
29. heart
30. lung
31. brain point
32. clavicle
33. nose
34. testis (ovary)
35. forehead
36. tongue
37. eye
38. internal ear
39. tonsil

Ear massage

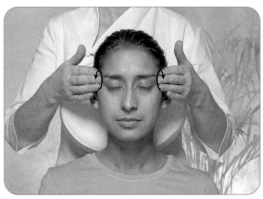

Gentle friction on the temples is very soothing

9 Eyebrow squeeze

Using your thumb and first finger, squeeze and release along the eyebrows from medial to lateral, three times. This releases tension in the corrugator supercili muscles.

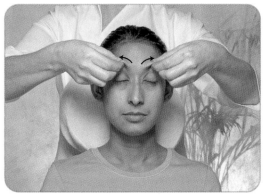

Eyebrow squeeze

10 Effleurage

Sweep across the face again, as in step 1.

Effleurage

11 Holding

Gently hold in three positions for five seconds: hands along the jawline; covering the eyes; and along the forehead. Gently squeeze inwards with palms when on the forehead.

Gently holding the face

The shoulder massage

The next part of the massage works on the shoulders. Many people hold a lot of tension in this area.

12 Linking effleurage

Place your hands on top of the head and lightly but briskly sweep down to the shoulders three times, before resting your hands on the shoulders.

13 Effleurage

Holding the top of the client's left shoulder, place the palm of your right hand on their right shoulder blade and make six large, clockwise circles around the right shoulder with medium pressure. Repeat on the left side with anti-clockwise circles.

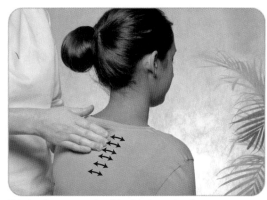

Friction between shoulder blade and spine

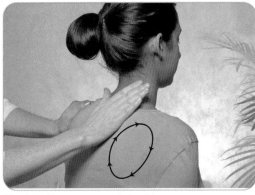

Circular effleurage around shoulders

14 Friction

Continue on the left, applying friction (side to side or circular) with finger pads between the shoulder blade and the spine and out along the top of the shoulder. Repeat, using the heel of your hand and then your fist. Repeat all on the right side.

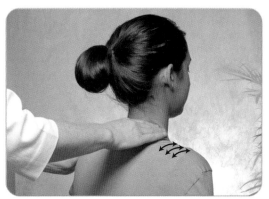

Friction on top of shoulders

15 Rubbing

With your whole hand, rub firmly and briskly all over both shoulders.

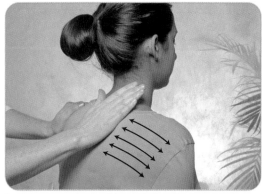

Rubbing upper back with whole hand

16 Kneading across shoulders

Use medium pressure to push forward with the heels of your hands up and over shoulders in three places, working from the corners of the shoulders towards the neck. Anchor your thumbs behind the neck and draw the muscles back with your fingers as you work out along the same area. Repeat twice more.

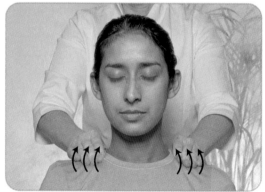

Kneading across shoulders

17 Freestyle kneading

Thoroughly knead the muscles on top of the shoulders and between the scapulae – experiment with your fingers, thumbs, fist, knuckles, forearms etc. You can also use a massage tool (see Chapter 7). Most people have tension in this region, which you can release.

18 Percussion

Keeping wrists loose, carry out hacking, champi (avoiding bony areas) and cupping across both shoulders.

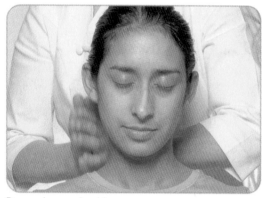

Percussion on shoulders

19 Neck stretch

Tilt the head gently to one side and support with your forearm and hand. Using the other forearm, gently and slowly sweep out across the neck from below the ear to the corners of the shoulders three times, easing pressure as you approach the bony area. Repeat on other side.

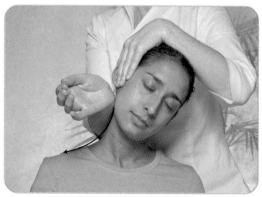

Stretching the neck

an indian head massage treatment

Massage of arms and hands

Massage of the whole arm and hands is very beneficial, especially for those who spend hours working on computer keyboards.

20 Relaxing the arms

Crouch or kneel down at one side and bring the client's arm down by their side. Holding at the wrist, shake gently to release tension and quickly roll the arm between your hands as you work down to the fingers, three times.

21 Compression

Holding the arm between both hands with thumbs pointing towards shoulder, slowly squeeze and release, working down to the wrist, three times.

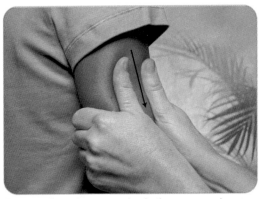

Compression releases tension in the arm muscles

22 Hand and wrist massage (dorsal)

Supporting the hand with your fingers, stroke up between metacarpals with your thumbs. Stroke all around wrist and press into the webbing between the thumb and index finger. This acupressure point is wonderful for relieving all types of pain, but is contraindicated in pregnancy.

Wrist and hand massage (dorsal)

23 Hand and wrist massage (palmar)

Turn hand over and stretch the palm by interlocking your little fingers with the client's little finger and thumb. Support with your other fingers underneath and open the client's hand to stretch the palm while your stroke it outwards using your thumbs. Stroke all around the carpal bones of the wrist.

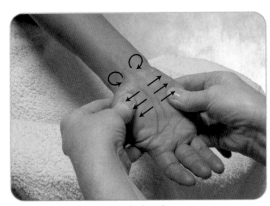

Wrist and hand massage (palmar)

24 Finger massage

Hold palm down in one hand and squeeze all over first finger. Rotate finger twice in each direction, then make a fist and stretch finger gently between two of your fingers. Repeat for each finger; then massage thumb and muscles at base of thumb deeply and thoroughly. Rest hand on client's lap and repeat on other side.

Massaging the fingers

25 Petrissage of upper arms

With the pads of your fingers, make small circular movements from the elbows to the top of the arms, working on the front, back and sides. Work on both arms together.

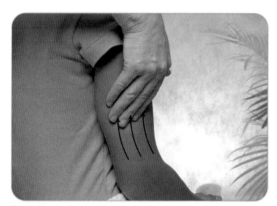
Petrissage of upper arms

Neck massage

The next part of the massage moves on to the neck. It is important not to use excessive pressure in this area.

26 Effleurage

Standing at the side with one hand on the client's forehead, tilt the head slightly back and use the thumb and fingers of your other hand to apply gentle, sweeping effleurage at the back of neck for about one minute.

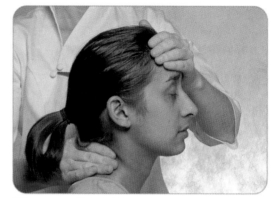
Effleurage on the neck

27 Friction

With one hand on the forehead, apply friction with the finger pads of your other hand up the side of the neck and under the occipital bone to the krikatika marma. Use gentle pressure on the vidhura marma (below mastoid process) but increase pressure going towards the krikatika to relieve muscular tension. Repeat twice more before doing other side.

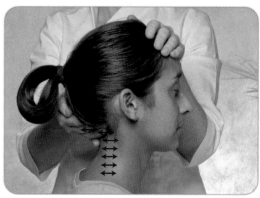
Neck and occipital friction

28 Occipital rubbing

With one hand on the client's forehead, tilt the head forward and rub the base of the skull with the heel of your other hand. Use side-to-side and up-and-down motions.

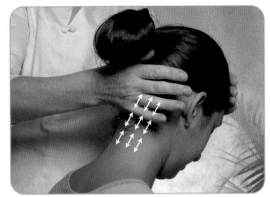

Rubbing under the occiput

Scalp massage

Untie long hair for this stage.

29 Effleurage

Standing behind the client, effleurage all over the right side of the head with the ball of the hand, starting behind the ear and finishing by ruffling the hair on top of the head. Repeat on left side. Repeat twice more on each side.

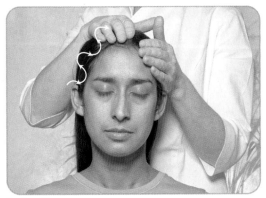

Scalp effleurage

30 Friction

Support the left side of head with your left hand and using the finger pads of your right hand, friction all over the right side of the head with medium pressure. Then apply friction to the other side.

Scalp friction

31 Whole-hand friction

Standing behind the client with both your hands above the ears and your fingers facing forward, apply friction to slowly move the scalp up and down three times. Move both your hands up and repeat, then repeat again at the top of the head. Move to the side of the client, placing one hand at the hairline and your other hand on the occiput and apply

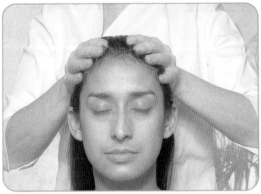

Whole-hand friction

friction again three times in three places, moving towards the top of the head.

32 Ruffling

Keeping light contact with the scalp and your wrists loose, use open fingers of one or both of your hands to ruffle the hair from all angles.

33 Plucking

With your fingers outstretched, gently bring them down on the client's head and spring them off, bringing your fingers and thumb together. Land in a different position with your fingers again outstretched. Repeat this energetic movement all over the head.

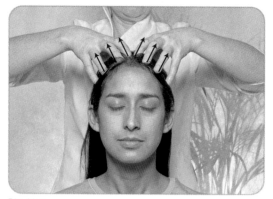

Plucking

34 Stroking

Standing behind the client, place one hand on top of the head with your fingers pointing forward and gently stroke back, following with the other hand in a wave-like motion as you stroke the hair six times with each hand. Comb through with your fingers if the client's hairstyle is appropriate.

35 Percussion

Use the flat of your fingers to perform tabla all over the head; then light hacking and champi.

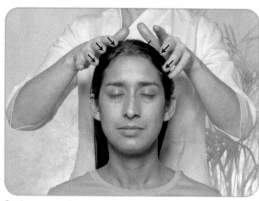

Scalp percussion

36 Hair tugging

Supporting one side of the head, grab fistfuls of hair at the roots with other hand and tug from side to side, keeping your hand close to the scalp. Do this in several places and repeat on other side. You can also take fistfuls of the hair with both hands and squeeze at the roots without tugging as you work all over the head.

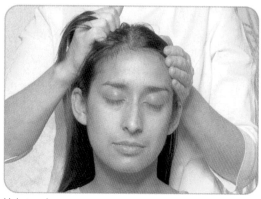

Hair tugging

37 Compression

With your elbows apart, lightly interlace your fingers and cup your hands towards the front of the client's head. Gently press your hands into the sides of the head, lifting the scalp. Hold for a few seconds, release slightly and

an indian head massage treatment

repeat twice more. Repeat with your hands above the ears and then behind the ears.

Scalp compression

38 Shampooing

Spread your thumbs and fingers over the scalp, making small circular movements to 'shampoo' with medium pressure. Work with your thumbs around the occipital area.

Shampooing

Chakra balancing

To balance the three upper chakras, stand behind your client, interlock your fingers and place them about 5 cm in front of the chakra. Take three deep breaths in each position, visualising the colour of the chakra as you

inhale and thinking of its mantra (sound) as you exhale. (See also Chapter 2.)

1 Throat chakra (Vissuda): Colour – Sky Blue; Sound – HAM

2 Brow/Third Eye chakra (Ajna): Colour – Indigo; Sound – OM

3 Crown chakra (Sahasrara): Colour – Purple or White/Gold; Sound – OM

Chakra balancing

Finishing procedure

It is important to take the time to finish the treatment well.

- Place hands on top of head and stroke down several times to shoulders and down arms before slowly removing hands.

- If client wishes to have oil applied to the scalp, it can be done now. (See Chapter 4 for how to apply oil to the scalp.)

- When you have finished, check that the client is comfortable before washing your hands and offering a glass of water.

- Record the client's feelings and make a note of any skin or other reactions, as well as any points to consider for future treatments (e.g. areas where tension was observed which may need more work at another time). Give aftercare advice to maintain effects of the treatment.

General homecare recommendations

As well as giving specific aftercare advice to each client depending on their individual condition, you can give these general, common-sense recommendations:

- Drink plenty of water to assist waste removal.
- Reduce intake of tea, coffee, alcohol, sugary foods, foods with added salt and eat a balanced diet with daily intake of fresh fruit and vegetables.
- Take regular exercise to improve blood and lymph circulation and strengthen cardiovascular system.
- Avoid restrictive clothing and sitting cross legged, both of which reduce efficiency of blood and lymph flow.
- Avoid harsh products and check diet if the hair is in poor condition.
- Get adequate sleep and make time for relaxation and enjoyment.

FAQs

My hands are quite rough and I am worried it may make massage of the face uncomfortable. What can I do about this?

Take care of your hands, especially if you use them to make a living. Wear protective gloves when washing up and use hand cream regularly. To keep your hands smooth, pour a teaspoonful of olive oil (or any other vegetable oil) and a half teaspoon of sugar or salt into the palm of one hand. Massage thoroughly all over both hands for a few minutes. Wash off and your hands will feel silky smooth. Do this once a week to keep your hands in top condition.

Can I use an on-site massage chair to do Indian Head Massage?

The treatment is generally done on a straight-backed chair but some therapists adapt the treatment for an on-site massage chair as they find it suits some clients.

Is it enough to work on the upper three chakras? What about the other chakras?

The chakras worked upon in Indian Head Massage are the higher chakras, with the crown regarded as the master chakra, controlling energy in all the other chakras. Balancing these chakras can bring the energy of the whole body back into harmony. Many people comment on the positive feelings they experience after chakra balancing.

What are some of the side effects of Indian head massage and why do they occur?

Massage encourages body systems to function more efficiently, in particular the lymphatic and circulatory systems. This results in speeding up waste removal and elimination of toxins. Some effects of massage may occur for a few days following treatment. This is referred to as a 'healing crisis' and should be viewed as the body getting rid of waste. Some of the following may be experienced:

- increase in micturition (urination) due to stimulation of circulation
- increase or other changes in bowel movements due to stimulation of the parasympathetic nervous system and more efficient elimination of waste
- headaches or light–headedness due to increased circulation and elimination of toxins
- increase in mucus from nasal passages as sinuses are draining following facial massage
- change in sleep pattern (usually increased, due to relaxation effects)
- increased thirst, due to increased urination
- increase in appetite, due to increase in metabolic rate
- relief of discomfort in muscles and joints; occasionally muscles can ache post-treatment as lactic acid is being released
- feeling of relaxed alertness, due to increase in blood flow to the brain.

casestudy

The following case study was sent to us by Kim, who uses an on-site massage chair:

"While working as a nurse with cancer patients, I witnessed the many benefits of touch and decided to train in several therapies, including Indian Head Massage. After visiting a farmer's market in town, I realised this would be an ideal place to advertise my business. I booked a stand and set off with my on-site massage chair, a bench for waiting clients and a home-made sign. It was a big success and I ended up doing 16 mini treatments on the first day. My three children come along and they love the buzz of the market. Between clients, they get the chair ready and take payment while I clean my hands with anti-bacterial gel. They now understand the value of money as they calculate things they want by how many treatments I give! I get clients to read a list of contraindications before treatment and find the on-site massage chair very useful, as some people are self-conscious in a public place and this way their face cannot be seen while I work on their shoulders and arms. By the time they sit up for the head massage, they are so chilled out, they don't care where they are and I usually have a queue waiting on the bench! I have regulars who return every weekend and have now gained a client base who come for longer treatments in my clinic."

an indian head massage treatment

self-care

I ndian Head Massage is quite physically demanding. It is important to pay attention to self-care so that clients receive optimum treatment without therapists causing undue wear and tear on their joints, or feeling too tired. As we age, the connective tissue between our joints gradually degenerates and this can lead to osteoarthritis, a disorder characterised by stiffness and pain. Looking after the joints is of particular importance to therapists.

It is also important for therapists to look after their general health and to get a fair reward for their work.

Areas for consideration include:

- ☙ the right equipment
- ☙ work scheme
- ☙ posture and joints
- ☙ nutrition
- ☙ exercise
- ☙ reaping a fair reward.

The right equipment

The equipment needed to give an Indian Head Massage is detailed in Chapter 6, but the following items are of particular importance for the care of the therapist.

Chair

This should preferably be a gas-lift chair, easily adjusted to suit the height of the client and the therapist. If the chair is too high, or too low, it can put pressure on muscles and joints and adversely affect the therapist's back, shoulders, neck and arms. The chair should have no arms, to allow easy access to the client. The client may feel more comfortable with a pillow placed on their lap to support their arms.

Indian Head Massage is best done on a height adjustable chair

Supports

Some techniques require a cushion or rolled-up towel to support the head. The ideal cushion is firm, small, and oval-shaped with washable covers (for hygiene). This type is available from therapy suppliers (see the 'Useful contacts' section in 'Where to go from here' at the end of this book). If the pillow is too soft, the therapist has to lean forward to support the head, putting pressure on their own back and shoulders. If the cushion is too large, the therapist has to reach around it to enable them to reach the face, again putting pressure on their shoulders and back.

A cushion and massage tools for Indian head massage

Work scheme

Be realistic about how many clients you can treat in a day and over consecutive days. A therapist's desire to help people makes it difficult to say 'no', but it is vital to keep your own muscles and joints in good heath. The amount of massage that can be done in one day varies from person to person. Therapists should take note of levels of fatigue and of aching muscles in the arms, shoulders, back and neck or sore joints in the hands and devise a suitable work scheme that won't leave them exhausted.

For therapists who wish to make a full-time living out of massage, it is preferable to learn a range of therapies, as each one will be physically different to perform, so will place strain on one particular set of muscles. Reflexology, face treatments and ear candling are all highly effective treatments that are performed from a seated position.

Posture and joints

Performing regular massage can strain muscles and joints so it is crucial to pay attention to how you stand and bend. Work out an optimum standing position so you are comfortable and able to bend your elbows and knees when necessary to exert pressure on the client. If you are too near the client, it is not possible to use your body weight to help with pressure, and if you are too far away, you will be forced to stretch unnecessarily. Keep your shoulders relaxed at all times. Be realistic – if the client asks for more pressure and you are working within your limit, tell them that this is your maximum pressure.

An alternative way to work the client's shoulders is to use a massage tool. This is a great way to loosen muscles and apply more pressure without putting undue strain on your own body. (See the 'Useful products' section in 'Where to go from here' at the end of this book.)

Nutrition

Just as plants draw nourishment from the earth and will not thrive if the soil is poor, if our bodies are poorly nourished, the signs soon become evident.

casestudy

Janna, a qualified naturopath who is also a massage therapist, offers the following advice to fellow therapists.

'As massage therapists, we use our bodies a lot. If the body is not being properly nourished, it will soon feel sluggish and tired, and physical exercise (for example giving massage) will only make us feel worse. Good nutrition boosts the immune system, making us less susceptible to colds or other viruses so that we don't have to miss days off work. It will nourish our spirit, too! This is just as important as nourishing our bodies, as studies have shown that we are more susceptible to illness when our spirits are low. The spirit also needs nourishing if we see a lot of clients, some of whom can be very draining.

What we should be eating is based on what I call the 'Stone-Age diet'. We evolved to our current human state relatively recently (in evolutionary terms) when there was no technology and Homo sapiens lived as hunter-gatherers. There hasn't been enough time for our bodies to adapt to our current lifestyles and diets, as this type of adaptation takes thousands of years. So ideally, our diet should be as close to what we imagine Stone Age Man's diet was. He would eat whatever was in season: nuts, berries, fruit, mushrooms, occasionally meat or fish (organic of course!), leaves, roots, rarely milk (and never wheat, as they didn't grow crops at all). We can also eat pulses and other cereals (e.g. millet, quinoa or rice). Of course, we all know this kind of diet is very difficult (if not impossible) to follow in our type of civilisation. But it is worth referring back to for guidance as much as we can. To encourage good health we can also:

- drink fresh vegetable and fruit juices regularly. Organic foods should be used as much as possible, as otherwise we are giving ourselves more of the chemicals we need to get rid of!
- ensure we drink enough water, but not excessive amounts. If the diet is full of cellular matter like vegetables and fruits, there is quite a lot of water there already, so it should depend on what is eaten.
- eat enough fibre – vegetable fibre is better than cereal-based fibre, as our digestive tracts are not designed for this
- have 'superfoods' like spirulina or chlorella if and when we are going down with a cold or flu, or if our diet has been inadequate.'

Nutritional supplements

In an ideal world, getting all the goodness we need from diet alone might be possible, but unfortunately, due to environmental pollution, chemicals and poor soil conditions this is not always the case. Adding good-quality nutritional supplements to the modern diet can help to counteract some of these effects. However, if you are pregnant, taking regular medication, or have any concerns about your health, you should consult your medical practitioner or a qualified nutritionist for advice rather than indiscriminately taking supplements that may not be right for you. As well as a top-quality multivitamin/

multimineral supplement, there are other supplements that can help to keep joints supple and flexible.

Essential fatty acids

Essential fatty acids (EFAs) are so called because they are essential for the structure of every cell membrane as well as maintenance of healthy joints, circulation and heart function. The body cannot make its own supply, so we need to get EFAs from food or supplements. EFAs fall into two groups: Omega 3, which is found in oily fish (e.g. tuna, mackerel, sardines, salmon) as well as linseeds and walnuts and Omega 6, found in nuts and seeds, such as sunflower and pumpkin seeds. Good-quality supplements of evening primrose and borage oil provide Omega 6 in a specially converted form known as gamma linoleic acid (GLA). Hemp seeds contain GLA and Omega 3.

These foods contain essential fatty acids

Glucosamine sulphate

This substance is a major building block of the complex proteins that form part of the structure of cartilage. It plays a vital role in everyday mobility and smooth working of cartilage, tendons and ligaments and aids the production of synovial fluid around joints. Glucosamine sulphate is naturally made in the body, but it is thought that larger quantities are needed when joints are damaged. Studies indicate that a mixture of glucosamine and chondroitin is the most effective. Chondroitin is commonly found in dietary supplements. The most usual form, chondroitin sulphate, decreases the activity of enzymes that break down cartilage and attracts water to joints.

Methylsulfonylmethane (MSM)

MSM is necessary for the structure of every cell in our bodies. It is a naturally occurring organic compound and one of the major building blocks of cartilage. It is present in small amounts in food and beverages. Cow's milk is the most abundant source of MSM; other sources include coffee, tomatoes, tea, Swiss chard, corn and alfalfa. Supplements are also available.

Exercise

The ideal type of exercise is that which stretches muscles and increases stamina. Yoga and Pilates are both excellent. Yoga, which means 'union', is a philosophy and discipline applied to the development of mind, body, and spirit. Through the practice of a variety of body positions (asanas) and centring of mind and breath in a meditative way, the practitioner increases body awareness,

Stretching exercises release tension, increase flexibility and calm the mind

posture, flexibility and calmness of mind and spirit.

Pilates is a technique developed in the 1920s by the German-American Joseph H. Pilates. Its focus is on improving flexibility and strength for the overall body without building bulk. The strength training movements involve co-ordinated breathing techniques, awareness of the spine, core strength and flexibility. The outcome of Pilates training is improved posture and a balanced body that is strong and supple. As it involves concentration and coordination of breath and movement, Pilates helps to balance mind and body.

Reaping a fair reward

People who train as complementary therapists are usually those with a caring nature who enjoy nurturing others. In our teaching we come across many such caring people who sometimes have difficulty in charging for their treatments. However, if you decide to make your living in this way, it is important to earn enough to live comfortably. When deciding how much to charge for your services, bear in mind the time, money and effort put into learning your skills. Look at what others in your area are charging when deciding on your fees and remember it is more difficult to increase your fees than to reduce them, so don't start too low! If your prices are too low, it may be assumed that you are not as skilled as someone who is charging more than you.

Self-massage

Massage has many wonderful effects on the physical and mental health of the person being massaged and fortunately, you have your very own massage therapist with you at all times – your hands! Most of us practise the art of self-massage unconsciously, whether rubbing our forehead or temples to relieve a headache, or scrubbing down in the shower. You can use self-massage to energise yourself in the morning or unwind in the evening.

Here are a few of our favourite self-massage techniques.

Relax your shoulders

Shrug your shoulders, bring them close to your ears for five seconds, then relax them down, feeling the tension ebb away. Repeat twice more. Squeeze and knead one shoulder firmly with the opposite hand, then change sides and repeat.

Relieve your neck

Your neck can hold a lot of tension that may restrict the flow of blood to your head, leading to headaches and lack of concentration, so massage here is very beneficial.

Hold the back of your neck with one hand and squeeze firmly to ease muscle tension. Lift your chin slightly and place both hands either side of the back of your head. Using your thumbs, firmly press into the base of the skull, supporting your head with your fingers. Start behind the ears and work in towards the middle of the neck, directing the pressure upwards. You can also apply friction in the area.

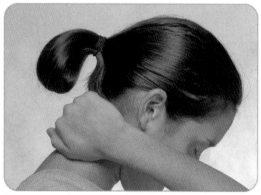

You can massage your own neck to relieve tension

Relax your face

Place your hands over your face, with your fingers on your forehead and the heels of your hands on your chin. Hold for five seconds, then slowly and gently draw them out towards your ears as you imagine all the tension dissolving from your face.

Soothe your eyes

Put the heels of your hands into your eye sockets and hold for a few seconds while you enjoy the darkness; then slowly glide your hands out to the sides. Repeat a few times. If your eyes feel tired from staring at your computer all day, rub your hands together vigorously until you feel them warming up; then cup one hand over each eye, feeling the heat soothe your eyes.

This exercise is great for eyestrain

Open your sinuses

Place the pads of your second or third fingers between your eyebrows, press down and rub outwards, tracing your brow line as you go. Repeat from the mid-line of the forehead and at the hairline. Then place the pads of your fingers either side of the bridge of your nose and apply friction as you work down the sides of the nose. Use your fingers to massage your cheekbones, making small circles, starting at the centre of your face and moving out toward your ears. Finally, place your thumbs on your temples and massage them in small circles. This also relieves tension headaches.

Massage your head

To drain away tension and leave you feeling relaxed and alert, place your hands on your scalp, spreading your fingers and thumbs to cover as wide an area as possible. Gently rotate them as you breathe deeply through your nose to promote good circulation. Most of our breathing is shallow so bringing in more oxygen helps to relieve fatigue and tension. Work your hands all over your scalp from your hairline to the nape of your neck and then reverse the direction. To keep your hair in top condition, you can also do this with your favourite oil.

Soothe your soles

If you practise massage, you will be on your feet most of the time so it's important to look after them. Sit in a comfortable position so you can easily reach your feet (e.g. cross-legged on the floor). Working on one foot at a time, hold your heel with one hand and with the other hand, massage each toe thoroughly. Gradually move down to the ball of your foot and knead this for a few minutes; then slowly work over your sole and down to your heel. You can use your favourite lotion to keep your feet soft, or apply sesame oil at night, which calms the nervous system and promotes good sleep. There are lots of acupressure points on the feet that can benefit the whole body.

An ancient Indian quote says:

'Diseases do not go near one who massages his feet before sleeping, just as snakes do not approach eagles.'

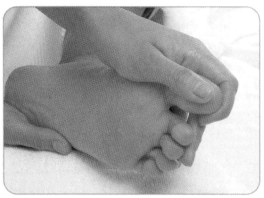
Massaging your feet has many health benefits

Pamper your hands

If you use your hands regularly it is important to take good care of them with a daily massage.

Apply your favourite lotion and start by clasping your fingers and rubbing the heels of your hands together in a circular motion. With your hands still clasped, use one thumb to massage the area just below your other thumb, moving towards the centre of the palm. Repeat with the other hand. Release your fingers and use your thumbs (on palm) and index fingers (on back of the hands) to knead your palms, wrists, and the webbing between your fingers. With one hand, gently pull each finger of the other hand. Finish by using your thumb and index finger to pinch the webbing between your other thumb and index finger. There are lots of acupressure points on the hands that can benefit the whole body.

FAQs

Can I prescribe nutritional supplements to my clients?

It is fine to offer basic common-sense nutritional advice such as encouraging clients to drink more water, cut down on processed or fast foods, eat more fresh and nutritious foods and give up smoking and excess alcohol. However, unless you are a qualified nutritionist, you should not prescribe nutritional supplements to your clients.

My friends and family expect free treatments and I am worried about making a living as a therapist. How should I approach this?

If you wish to make a living as a therapist you need to adopt a professional approach and you will find people appreciate and respect this. Ensure your treatment environment is impeccable. Always look professional when giving treatments, even to friends and family. Prepare literature giving details of your qualifications, treatments offered, prices, dates and times available. Always carry business cards (see 'Useful products') to give to anyone who asks about your work and if they begin discussing their health problems, suggest they make an appointment to see you. You may wish to offer discounts to friends and family, but free treatments are not advisable as people could take you for granted. We recommend that free treatments should be restricted to charitable causes.

anatomy and physiology

When giving Indian Head Massage, it is important to have knowledge of the body structures you are working on. Anatomy (from the Greek 'ana-temnein', to cut up) deals with the structure and organisation of living things, while physiology is the study of the mechanical, physical, and biochemical functions of living organisms – in this case, the human body. Practitioner training courses cover anatomy and physiology in detail (see the 'Useful contacts' section in 'Where to go from here' at the end of this book).

Let's begin with what we first observe – the outer wrapping!

The skin

Skin, hair and nails are often referred to as the 'integument', a protective outer covering. The skin is the largest body organ, with an average area of 2.2 square metres. The thickness varies: the eyelids are the thinnest and the soles of the feet the thickest. Skin can absorb small molecules contained in essential oils and certain other chemical substances.

The skin is composed of two layers: the outer epidermis and the dermis underneath.

Beneath the dermis is the subcutaneous layer, normally thicker in females than males. It is composed of fatty tissue as well as elastic fibres, making it flexible as well as reducing heat loss through the skin and protecting underlying organs from injury.

The epidermis

The epidermis is made up of five layers.

The stratum germanitivum

This is the deepest layer (the basal layer). Its lower surface is attached to the dermis, from which it receives nutrients through blood vessels. Here, the cells are living and mitosis (cell division) occurs. As new cells are produced, older cells are gradually pushed upwards, taking an average of 28 days to reach the upper layers of the epidermis (this time period increases with age). Melanin, a pigment that protects skin from the harmful effects of ultra-violet sunlight, is formed in special cells called 'melanocytes' in this layer. Loss of melanocytes in areas of the skin results in vitiligo, a condition that produces whitish patches on the skin. Chloasma, which is associated with hormonal changes, causes brown pigmentation marks, often on the face. Albinism is a rare, inherited disorder characterised by a total or partial lack of melanin in the skin.

The stratum spinosum

This layer (also known as the 'prickle cell' layer) houses the cells immediately above the basal layer. These rows of cells are still living and capable of mitosis. Their membranes, however, are beginning to split, giving the cells a prickly appearance when viewed under a microscope.

The stratum granulosum

In the 3–5 rows of this granular layer, cells become flattened and the nucleus begins to disintegrate as cells lose fluid and fill with granules of a substance called keratohyalin. This is the first stage in their transformation into a tough, fibrous, waterproof protein called keratin.

The stratum lucidum

The cells in the stratum lucidum (or clear layer) are transparent, small, tightly packed, and have no nucleus. This layer is very thin in facial skin but thick on the soles and palms. It is thought to be the barrier zone, controlling transmission of water through the skin.

The stratum corneum

The stratum corneum (or horny layer) is composed of 25–30 rows of keratinised cells packed tightly together, the outer layers of which are constantly being shed and replaced from below. Keratin keeps the skin water-

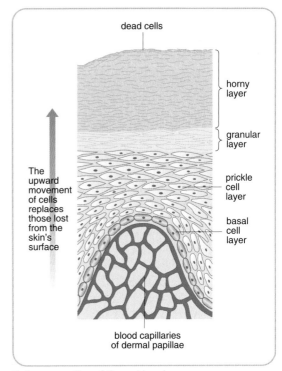

Cell regeneration of the epidermis

proof, preventing the body from becoming waterlogged, and keeps out harmful chemical substances. It also prevents the entry of bacteria, which could cause infection.

The dermis

The dermis contains tough, flexible connective tissue, composed of collagen, providing strength and elastin, which gives the skin resilience and elasticity. Fibroblast cells manufacture collagen and elastin. With age, these cells slow down production, leading to loss of strength and elasticity in the skin. Other cells found here include mast cells, which secrete histamine in allergic reactions, and white blood cells that fight infection.

Nerve endings

The upper region of the dermis contains nerve endings for touch, pain, heat, cold and pressure. These send messages to the central nervous system about what is going on outside the body and on the skin surface.

Sebaceous glands

A little deeper are structures such as the sebaceous glands, which open into the hair follicles. These are more numerous on the scalp and face, particularly on the forehead, chin, cheeks and nose. They secrete sebum, a natural oil that moisturises and conditions skin and hair. Sebum and sweat mix on the surface of the skin to form an 'acid mantle', which is a protective barrier against certain bacteria, fungi and viruses. Sebum production increases after puberty, as the hormones oestrogen and testosterone activate the sebaceous glands. Excess sebum may result in comedones (blackheads), milia (whiteheads) or acne if sebaceous glands become inflamed. Sebum production decreases with age, particularly in women, whose oestrogen supplies diminish after menopause. UV rays from sunlight change a chemical found in sebum into Vitamin D. This passes into the bloodstream and is important for the growth of strong teeth and bones.

Sweat glands

Sweat glands are tube-like ducts which rise up through the epidermis, ending at the surface to form a pore. Eccrine sweat glands are found all over the body and excrete waste through sweating. This cools on evaporation, helping to regulate body temperature. Apocrine glands found in the underarms, genitals and breasts secrete fatty substances as well as salt and water, which react to air and can cause body odour.

Blood and lymph vessels

The dermis also contains fine blood and lymph vessels, which carry nutrients and allow removal of waste from the skin. When the body heats up (e.g. during exercise) blood vessels in the dermis dilate, allowing extra blood to the surface to lose heat. When we are cold, they constrict as blood moves in towards vital body organs. Stress reactions cause blood vessels in the skin to constrict as blood is diverted to the heart, lungs and muscles in 'fight or flight' situations. This reduces the supply of oxygen and nutrients to the skin and accounts for stress-related skin and hair disorders.

Hair follicles

Hair follicles, which are downward growths in the dermis, are found all over the body except on the lips, soles and palms. Cells move up the follicle from the hair bulb at its base, changing in structure to form a hair. Tiny muscles (the erector pili) attached to hair follicles cause hairs to stand erect when we are cold, trapping heat near the surface of the skin to warm us. Aggression or fright also contracts these muscles, leading to the appearance of 'goose bumps'.

In the next section, we look in more detail at the structure of the hair.

anatomy and physiology

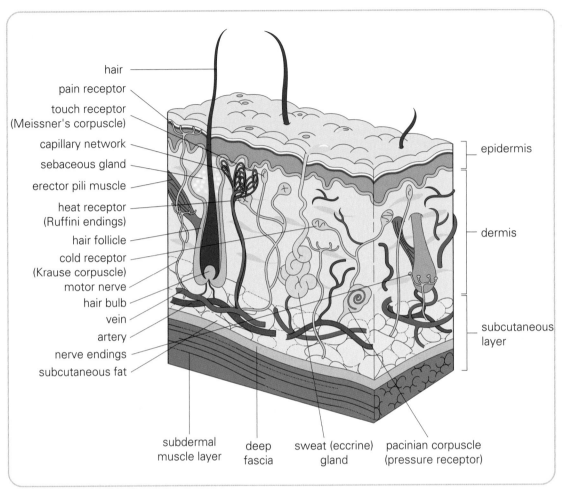

Cross-section of the skin

The hair

The main function of hair is protection. It guards the scalp from cold temperatures, injury and the sun's rays; the eyes from foreign particles; and the ear canal and nostrils from insects and inhaled particles. Each hair is composed of a shaft, most of which projects above the surface of the skin, and the root below.

The shaft of coarse hairs, such as those on the scalp, consists of three parts: the medulla, the cortex and the cuticle.

- The medulla is composed of large, loosely connected cells containing keratin and air spaces. Reflection of light through air spaces within the medulla determines the visible sheen and colour tone of hair.

- The cortex, which forms the bulk of the hair, is composed of long cells containing keratin and the pigment melanin, determining hair colour. This pigment can vary from brown-black to yellow-red. Hair turns grey and eventually white as pigment glands slow their production and eventually shut down.

❧ The outer cuticle consists of a single layer of thin, flat, keratinised cells overlapping like slates on a roof. These cells point upwards and interlock with the scale-like cells that line the inner root sheath of the follicle, which point downwards, securing the hair in place.

The hair root, which penetrates into the dermis and in some cases into the subcutaneous layer, also contains a medulla,

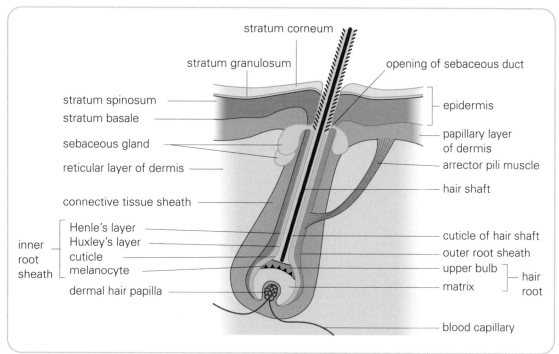

stratum corneum

stratum granulosum

opening of sebaceous duct

stratum spinosum

stratum basale

sebaceous gland

reticular layer of dermis

connective tissue sheath

inner root sheath

Henle's layer

Huxley's layer

cuticle

melanocyte

dermal hair papilla

epidermis

papillary layer of dermis

arrector pili muscle

hair shaft

cuticle of hair shaft

outer root sheath

upper bulb

matrix

hair root

blood capillary

Hair and follicle

cortex and cuticle, continuous with the hair shaft. Surrounding the root is the hair follicle, which consists of several layers:

❧ The inner root sheath is composed of three layers, the innermost of which interlocks with the hair cuticle, keeping the hair in place.

❧ The outer root sheath is a downward continuation of the epidermis. Near the surface it contains all the epidermal layers, while at the base of the follicle it contains only basal cells.

The base of each hair follicle is enlarged into an onion-shaped bulb, containing an indentation (papilla) filled with loose connective tissue and with blood capillaries, which nourish the growing hair. Hair growth originates from the central area of the bulb, the matrix, an area of active growth where cells undergo mitosis. These cells are then pushed upwards, where they fill with keratin to produce a hair that eventually projects from the open end of the follicle when older hairs are shed. Electrolysis and laser treatments destroy the hair bulb to prevent re-growth.

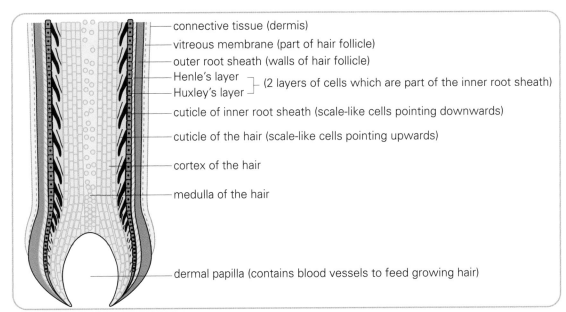

Labels:
- connective tissue (dermis)
- vitreous membrane (part of hair follicle)
- outer root sheath (walls of hair follicle)
- Henle's layer ⎤ (2 layers of cells which are part of the inner root sheath)
- Huxley's layer ⎦
- cuticle of inner root sheath (scale-like cells pointing downwards)
- cuticle of the hair (scale-like cells pointing upwards)
- cortex of the hair
- medulla of the hair
- dermal papilla (contains blood vessels to feed growing hair)

Cross-section of hair in the follicle

Hair growth

Hair grows in repeated cycles. One cycle can be broken down into three phases and each hair passes through each of the phases independent of neighbouring hairs.

Anagen phase

This is the active or growth phase, accounting for about 85 per cent of hair at any one time with different hairs at different stages of growth. Anagen can vary from between two and seven years for scalp hair, one or two months for eyebrows and between three and six weeks for eyelashes. In early anagen, a new hair bulb surrounds the nutrient-providing papilla and a hair begins to grow from living cells in the matrix. Anagen ends when the hair begins to separate from the papilla and no longer receives nutrients.

Catagen

This changing or transitional phase lasts about one or two weeks. Only one per cent of hairs are at this stage at any one time. The hair

is now fully grown and cell division has stopped. The hair has separated from the papilla and the follicle begins to shrink, cutting the hair off from its blood supply and from cells that produce new hair. Hairs at this stage are called 'club hairs' due to their club shape at the base.

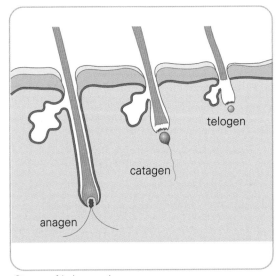

Stages of hair growth

Telogen

This 'resting' phase lasts about five or six weeks, during which time the hair does not grow but stays attached to the follicle while the papilla stays in a resting phase below. The resting hair will either fall out or be pushed out by a new hair growing underneath. Approximately ten or fifteen per cent of hairs are in this phase at any one time. At the end of telogen, the hair follicle re-enters the anagen phase: the papilla and base of the follicle join together again and a new hair begins to form. If the old hair has not already been shed, the new hair pushes it out and the growth cycle starts again.

Types of hair growth

Lanugo

From the Latin for 'down', this is the hair of the newborn infant, which is fine and soft. In premature infants it may be found all over the body but this is lost soon after birth. Lanugo is replaced by new hair that is stronger and more pigmented.

Vellus

This hair is soft, downy and almost invisible. It is found all over the body, except on the lips, palms and soles.

Terminal

Compared to vellus hair, terminal hair is longer and coarser, with deeper follicles. These hairs are found on the head, the eyebrows and the eyelashes and in the axillary and pubic regions.

Factors that affect hair growth

It is normal to lose between 80 and 100 hairs a day, but losing more than this can lead to hair thinning. Hair thinning can be due to a variety of causes.

Climate

Studies indicate that hair grows faster during spring and summer and slower during winter months in temperate regions. Excessive exposure to UV rays of the sun can dry out the scalp and hair so it is wise to use a sunscreen or to wear a hat for protection.

Diet

Two dietary factors that affect hair health are deficiencies of protein and iron. Protein is essential for cell growth and repair, while iron produces haemoglobin in the blood, which carries oxygen for growth and regeneration of all body cells. In Traditional Chinese Medicine (TCM), the hair is seen as an extension of the blood, and so reflects its state. Other nutrients for good hair health are essential fatty acids (EFAs) and Vitamins B complex and C, which nourish hair follicles. Smoking destroys Vitamin C and nicotine causes blood vessels to constrict, making it harder for nutrients to reach the skin and hair and for waste to be eliminated.

Genes

Androgenetic alopecia or 'male-pattern baldness' can be passed on through successive generations. Although it affects both men and women, women are less likely to develop full-blown androgenetic alopecia because the gene reacts to the androgen range of hormones (such as testosterone), which are more prevalent in males. Oestrogen, the equivalent dominant hormone in women, keeps the action of the gene in check until menopause, but after that a woman who carries the inherited gene may suffer hair loss.

Hormones

High androgen (male hormone) levels in a female can lead to polycystic ovarian syndrome, with symptoms such as hair loss, amenorrhoea, hirsutism (excess body and facial hair) or acne. Hair is sensitive to changes in thyroxin levels and gradual hair loss can result from hyposecretion of the thyroid. Hair can become greasier at puberty and during menstruation while a drop in oestrogen levels at menopause can lead to dry, coarse, brittle hair. There may be temporary hair loss during pregnancy, or after delivery, due to a drop in oestrogen levels.

Medication

Drugs that may cause temporary hair loss include chemotherapy (used in cancer treatment), anaesthetics, anticoagulants (used to thin the blood), retinoids (to treat acne and skin problems), beta-adrenergic blockers (to control blood pressure) and oral contraceptives. No one should stop taking prescribed medication without their doctor's advice, but dietary changes and some well-chosen supplements can really make a difference to hair and scalp condition.

Processing and chemicals

Perming and dyeing, as well as overuse of hair dryers and straighteners, can damage the hair, making it dry and brittle. Frequent use of shampoos and hair treatments full of detergents and chemicals can dry out the scalp. Treated water in swimming pools can also dry and irritate the scalp.

Shock

Shock has been known to cause hair to fall out as blood vessels in the skin constrict, starving the hair of vital nutrients. With extreme trauma, this can happen overnight.

Stress

Hair is one of the first places the body shows distress. When we are under stress, it is easy to let basic health habits go. We may end up eating badly and not getting enough sleep. Tension in the scalp restricts the flow of oxygen and nutrients to hair follicles.

Styling

Pony tails, plaits and braids put extra stress on hair roots and can cause hair loss. Hair is most fragile when wet and should not be brushed, but carefully combed through instead with a wide tooth comb and left to dry naturally, if possible.

Types of hair

To identify your hair type, pat a tissue on your hair the second day after washing. If it is slightly oily, you have normal hair; if nothing shows, your hair is dry; and if strands stick together, you have greasy hair.

Dry hair

Dry hair is usually due to under-active sebaceous glands but can also be caused by other factors like over-exposure to the sun and harsh products. Accumulated sebum can lead to dryness by blocking pores and preventing the oil getting to the surface. Dry hair needs

Excessive use of electrical hair equipment dries the hair

plenty of nourishment, so massage well with warm oil at least once a week (see Chapter 4). Use a mild shampoo, as harsh chemicals can strip hair of its outer protein layer, drying the scalp further. Avoid electric curlers, straighteners and dryers as these can break and split the hair.

Curly hair

This is usually dry, because oils produced in the scalp do not travel as easily down the hair shaft as they do with straight hair. Creamy, moisturising shampoos work best for this hair texture. It is best not to wash curly hair every day, as it may become dehydrated, frizzy and unmanageable. An alternative to shampooing is to rinse with water and follow with conditioner.

Oily hair

Oily hair is usually accompanied by oily skin and is due to excess sebum leaving the scalp and hair too oily. Oily hair looks greasy even after shampooing and attracts dirt easily, so needs regular washing, depending on individual comfort. Use oils and shampoos rich in neem and henna and rinse with lemon. Avoid foods high in saturated fats and increase intake of green leafy vegetables and fruit.

Fine hair

Fine hair is not necessarily thin hair, although the two often come together. With thin hair there are not many strands on the head but some people have thick hair that is considered 'fine' because it is silky and smooth, without the curls or roughness that provide texture. Fine hair grows from smaller, narrower follicles. It tends to lack volume, so conditioners and other products are best applied to the ends rather than roots to avoid weighing down the hair.

Balanced or normal hair

This hair type is shiny, well-balanced and does not dry out easily. To maintain this condition, a good diet and proper hair care are essential.

Muscles

Underneath the skin are the skeletal muscles. There are around 700 muscles in the body. In this section we look at the main muscles that are worked on in a typical Indian Head Massage session.

On top of the skull lies a strong tendon, the galea aponeurotica ('galea' means helmet in Latin and 'aponeurotica' means a flat tendon). Attached between this tendon and the skin above the eyes is the frontalis muscle, which draws the scalp forward, raises the eyebrows and wrinkles the forehead. At the back of the skull lies the occipitalis, between the occipital bone and galea aponeurotica, which draws the scalp backwards. Sometimes these muscles are considered together, as the occipitofrontalis.

The procerus muscle, which is a continuation of the frontalis, wrinkles at the bridge of the nose to express disgust. The corrugator supercili muscles raise the eyebrows and 'corrugate' the brow to express worry, anger or concentration.

The circular orbicularis oculi muscles surround the eyes and allow blinking and closing. A tiny muscle on each eyelid, the levator palpabrae, lifts the eyelids to open the eyes.

On the sides of the nose, the nasalis muscles compress and dilate the nostrils and the circular orbicularis oris surrounds and closes the mouth.

The zygomaticus muscles run from the zygomatic bone (cheekbone) to the corners of the mouth, drawing them upwards into a smile. The levator anguli oris is also involved in drawing back the corners of the mouth, while the levator labii superioris, thin bands of muscle running from eye to mouth, elevate the upper lip.

The triangular-shaped depressor anguli oris muscles (sometimes called the triangularis) pull down the corners of the mouth when we feel sad. The buccinator muscles in the cheeks enable sucking and blowing, while the *risorius* muscles draw the corners of the mouth out when grinning.

On the chin, the mentalis pulls the skin up when pouting and turns the lower lip outwards.

The muscles used for chewing are called muscles of mastication. The strong masseter muscles run from the maxilla (upper jaw) and cheekbone (zygomatic arch) to the lower jawbone (mandible) and can be felt when the teeth are clenched. The temporalis muscles which cover the temporal bones above the ears work with the masseter muscles to open and close the mouth. These muscles become very tight, especially in stressed people, so massage in this area is very important.

The deepest muscles in the cheeks are the wing-shaped pterygoids, which raise the mandible and allow it to move from side to side.

The broad, flat platysma covers the front of the neck, depressing the mandible and drawing the lower lip down when pouting.

The rope-like sternocleidomastoid muscles run up the sides of the neck. They flex the neck as well as rotating the head.

When leaning back to look upwards, the trapezius muscle contracts. This kite-shaped muscle covers the whole of the upper back, from the occipital bone along the cervical and thoracic vertebrae to attach to the clavicle, the acromium (the highest point on the shoulder) and spine of the scapula.

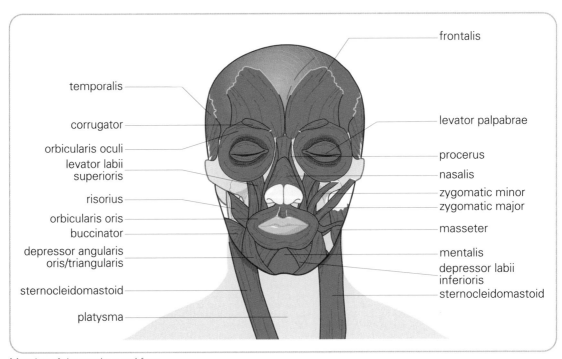

Muscles of the cranium and face

Beneath the trapezius are the rhomboids between the spine and the shoulder blades. These muscles often ache and are greatly alleviated by massage.

A ribbon-shaped group of muscles, the erector spinae, run all the way from the iliac and sacral bones in the pelvis to the occipital bone at the base of the skull, extending the vertebral column. The splenius cervicus and splenius capitis, which extend the neck and turn and twist the head when driving, are part of this group.

Capping the top of each shoulder is the triangular deltoid muscle, which contracts when the arm is abducted (lifted away from the body), while the biceps and triceps of the upper arm enable us to flex and extend at the elbow. Four deep muscles and their tendons form a nearly complete circle around the shoulder joint, providing strength and stability to keep the humerus (the upper arm bone) in place. They are the rotator cuff muscles: the supraspinatus, infraspinatus, teres minor and subscapularis. This is a common site of injury

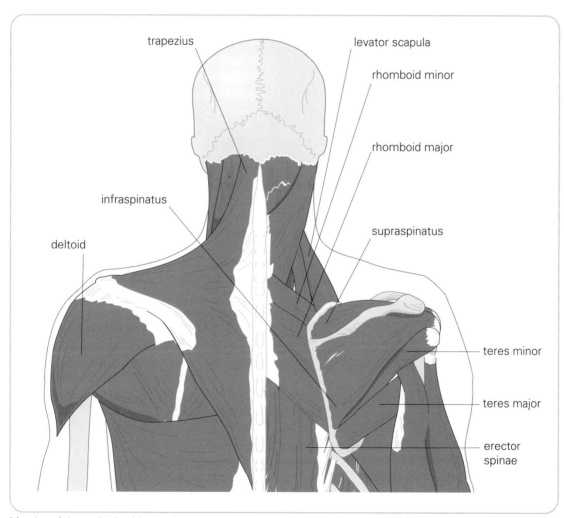

Muscles of the neck, shoulders and arms

for sports people such as basketball players or shot putters.

On the anterior forearm we have lots of flexor muscles running from elbow to hand, while at the back we have extensors – these muscles allow us to flex and extend our wrists and fingers.

Bones

The skull is made up of twenty-two bones, with eight forming the dome-shaped cranium and fourteen forming the face.

Cranial bones

The cranial bones consist of:

- ☙ one frontal bone forming the forehead, eye sockets and part of the nose

- ☙ one occipital bone at back of the skull with a large opening (the foramen magnum) through which the spinal cord passes into the skull to join the brain

- ☙ two parietal bones, which form the sides and roof of the cranium

- ☙ two temporal bones on each side of the head, with openings to the middle and inner ears

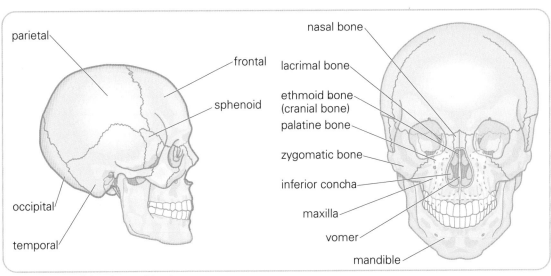

Bones of the skull (cranium and face)

- ☙ one butterfly-shaped sphenoid bone, forming the floor of the cranium and the temples

- ☙ one ethmoid bone at the roof of the nose, forming the supporting structures of the nasal cavities.

Facial bones

The facial bones consist of:

- ☙ one mandible, forming the lower jaw and connected to the temporal bone at the hinge-like temporomandibular joint (TMJ)

- two maxillae, forming the upper jaw, the front part of the hard palate, part of the side walls of the nose and floor of the eye sockets

- two palatine bones, forming the back part of the hard palate, part of the side walls of the nose and part of the floor of the eye sockets

- two small nasal bones forming the bridge of the nose

- two zygomatic bones forming the cheeks and sides of the eye sockets

- two tiny lacrimal bones on the inside walls of the eye sockets (a groove between the lacrimal bones and the nose forms a canal through which tears flow across the eyeball into the nasal cavity)

- two scroll-shaped inferior conchae ('turbinate bones'), which form a curved ledge along the inside walls of the nasal cavity, encouraging the turbulent circulation and filtration of air before it passes into the lungs

- one vomer bone, which joins the ethmoid bone to form the nasal septum, separating the two nostrils.

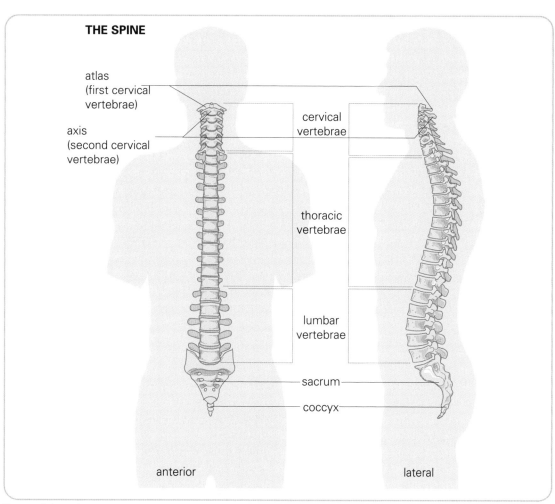

THE SPINE

atlas (first cervical vertebrae)

axis (second cervical vertebrae)

cervical vertebrae

thoracic vertebrae

lumbar vertebrae

sacrum

coccyx

anterior

lateral

Bones of the spine

Neck, shoulder and arm bones

Indian Head Massage works on the neck, shoulders and arms, so it is important to know the names of these bones. The spine or backbone is composed of 33 bones called vertebrae. By adulthood, five bones at the base of the spine (the sacrum) have fused into one and the four tail-bones (the coccyx) have also fused together. This is one reason why we lose our flexibility with age.

The seven bones in the neck are called cervical vertebrae ('cervix' is Latin for 'neck'). Below that, we have twelve thoracic vertebrae attached to the ribs and five large lumbar vertebrae in the lower back.

The shoulder girdle is the bony arch made up of two clavicles (collarbones) and two scapulae (shoulder blades). The humerus (upper arm bone) sits in a socket of the

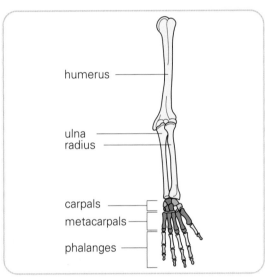

Bones of the arms and hand

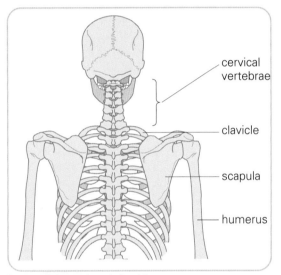

Bones of the neck and shoulders

scapula to form the most moveable joint in the body. It connects with the radius and ulna bones of the forearm at the elbow joint.

Eight small carpal bones form each wrist while five metacarpal bones form the palm of the hand and fourteen phalanges form the fingers and thumb.

The sinuses

The paranasal sinuses are cavities located inside bones of the skull. As well as giving resonance to the voice, the sinuses warm and moisten inhaled air and reduce the weight of the skull. Like the nose, they are lined with very fine, hair-like cilia. The function of the cilia is to move mucus produced by the sinuses towards the tiny holes that provide drainage into the nasal cavity.

The two maxillary sinuses are in the cheeks. The ethmoid sinuses are located around the bridge of the nose, behind and between the eyes. Both the maxillary and ethmoid sinuses are present at birth, while the frontal sinuses in the forehead do not develop until around seven years of age. The sphenoid sinuses are located deep in the face, behind the nose, and do not develop until adolescence.

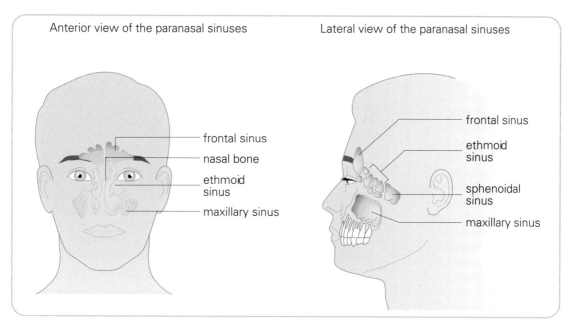

Anterior view of the paranasal sinuses

frontal sinus
nasal bone
ethmoid sinus
maxillary sinus

Lateral view of the paranasal sinuses

frontal sinus
ethmoid sinus
sphenoidal sinus
maxillary sinus

Anterior and lateral view of paranasal sinuses

Circulation

Oxygen and nutrients are supplied to body cells and waste is carried away through the combined efforts of the cardiovascular and lymphatic systems, sometimes collectively described as the 'circulatory system'. The average amount of blood in the human body is five litres and at any one time, approximately 20 per cent of this is circulating in the head area, feeding the brain and all the structures of the head.

The cardiovascular system

This system consists of the heart and the blood vessels (arteries and veins). Its main functions are to carry oxygen from air and nutrients from food to all body cells. Blood is pumped around the body by the heart, making a complete circuit in just over one minute. Bright red, oxygenated blood leaves the left side of the heart in a large artery called the aorta, which splits to form smaller arteries, supplying all areas of the body. These smaller arteries split even more, to form arterioles, and then branch out into capillaries, which have walls that are only one cell thick.

Oxygen, nutrients and fluid (plasma) exit through capillary walls and enter body cells, while waste products such as carbon dioxide and excess fluid are picked up. This leads to a change in the colour of blood, which now appears blue rather than bright red. The capillaries then unite to form small veins (venules), which eventually merge into the superior and inferior vena cava, two large veins that enter the right side of the heart. From here, the blood travels to the lungs in pulmonary arteries, where carbon dioxide is exchanged for oxygen before returning to the left side of the heart in pulmonary veins.

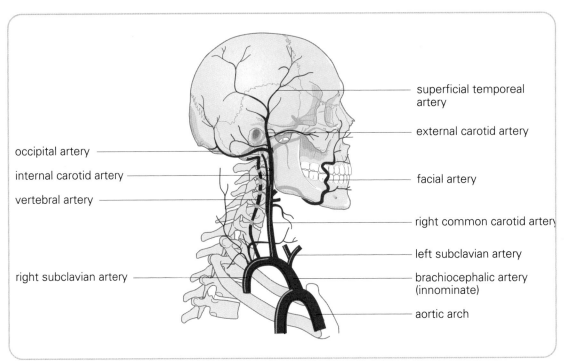

occipital artery

internal carotid artery

vertebral artery

right subclavian artery

superficial temporeal artery

external carotid artery

facial artery

right common carotid artery

left subclavian artery

brachiocephalic artery (innominate)

aortic arch

Arteries of the head and neck

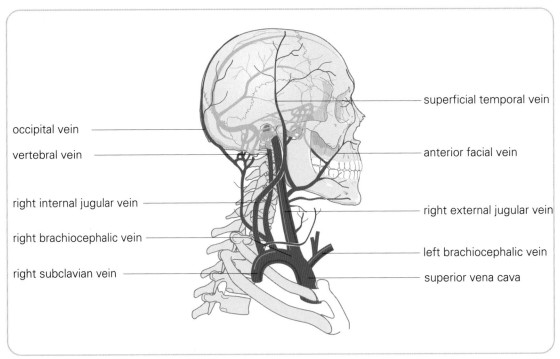

occipital vein

vertebral vein

right internal jugular vein

right brachiocephalic vein

right subclavian vein

superficial temporal vein

anterior facial vein

right external jugular vein

left brachiocephalic vein

superior vena cava

Veins of the head and neck

The lymphatic system

Lymph is a clear, straw-coloured fluid that starts out as plasma, flowing through the arteries carrying oxygenated blood and nutrients to supply body cells. Plasma leaks out of capillaries into tissue spaces between cells to become tissue fluid. This bathes the cells, providing oxygen and nutrients essential for energy, growth, and renewal as well as removing bacteria and waste. Some of the fluid is returned to blood capillaries, where it becomes plasma again in the veins, while excess fluid containing waste molecules too large to enter blood capillaries is drained into lymphatic capillaries which join together, forming larger vessels. The fluid is now called lymph. The lymph flows in a closed network of vessels in a system that is completely separate from the blood circulation.

To flow efficiently, the lymphatic system relies on movement of nearby muscles, for example, when breathing or walking. As muscles contract, they squeeze lymph along lymphatic vessels, which have valves to prevent it flowing back. Located at intervals along lymphatic vessels are bean-shaped organs called lymph nodes that contain lymphocytes, specialised white blood cells which destroy certain bacteria, viruses and other pathogens. These nodes filter lymph, cleaning it up before it eventually returns to the bloodstream through two lymphatic ducts that empty into subclavian veins in the neck. And so the cycle continues. At night, when the lymphatic system slows down, fluid builds up in the tissues, sometimes leading to facial puffiness first thing in the morning. Lack of physical exercise, as well as poor diet, pollution, and shallow breathing all restrict lymphatic drainage and slow the flow of lymph. This can manifest in the skin as spots, blackheads, and dry patches.

Massage speeds up blood and lymph circulation and helps the vessels get rid of waste that has not been removed naturally. There are important lymph nodes on the face and neck. Clients soon notice a difference in their complexion and general well-being when these nodes are stimulated through Indian Head Massage.

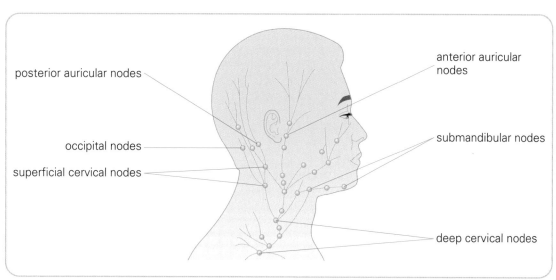

Lymph nodes of the head and neck

posterior auricular nodes

anterior auricular nodes

occipital nodes

submandibular nodes

superficial cervical nodes

deep cervical nodes

The nervous system

The nervous system is a control and communication system. It senses changes in the external environment and within the body, and responds to those changes through voluntary actions (such as closing a window when you feel cold) and involuntary actions (such as breathing). Around each hair follicle are nerve endings called 'hair root plexuses' that are sensitive to touch and respond if a hair shaft is moved. Thus Indian Head Massage can have a profound effect on the nervous system

and can be used to both stimulate and relax, depending on the techniques used.

The two divisions of the nervous system are the central nervous system, which incorporates the brain and spinal cord; and the peripheral nervous system, which incorporates twelve pairs of cranial nerves arising from the brain and thirty-one pairs of spinal nerves emerging from the spinal cord. Some of the peripheral nerves are sensory, relaying information from receptors located all over the body (including

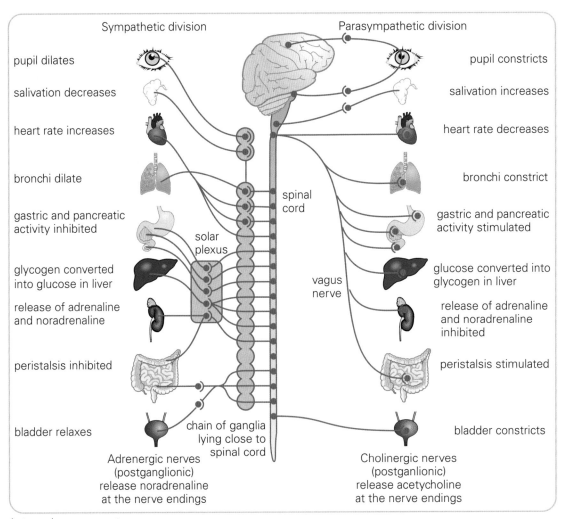

Sympathetic division   Parasympathetic division

pupil dilates   pupil constricts

salivation decreases   salivation increases

heart rate increases   heart rate decreases

bronchi dilate   spinal cord   bronchi constrict

gastric and pancreatic activity inhibited   solar plexus   gastric and pancreatic activity stimulated

glycogen converted into glucose in liver   vagus nerve   glucose converted into glycogen in liver

release of adrenaline and noradrenaline   release of adrenaline and noradrenaline inhibited

peristalsis inhibited   peristalsis stimulated

bladder relaxes   chain of ganglia lying close to spinal cord   bladder constricts

Adrenergic nerves (postganglionic) release noradrenaline at the nerve endings   Cholinergic nerves (postganlionic) release acetycholine at the nerve endings

Autonomic nervous system

each and every hair) to the central nervous system. Others are motor nerves, which carry information from the central nervous system, leading to voluntary or involuntary action by or within the body. There are also some mixed nerves, which contain both motor and sensory fibres, e.g. the nerves that enable the tongue to move as well as carry information to the brain about different tastes.

The peripheral nervous system is divided into two branches:

- the voluntary (somatic) nervous system
- the involuntary (autonomic) nervous system.

The somatic (voluntary) nervous system allows us to control some parts of the body, including the muscles, while the autonomic (involuntary) system operates without our conscious control. The autonomic branch of the peripheral nervous system is further subdivided into the sympathetic and parasympathetic nervous systems, which have opposing functions in the body.

The sympathetic nervous system is activated in times of stress, preparing the body for 'fight or flight'. Some of its effects include stimulation of the adrenal and sweat glands; increased heart and breathing rate; release of stored glucose into the blood to fuel the skeletal muscles for action; and decrease of blood flow to the skin, digestive, urinary and reproductive systems. These bodily changes enable us to deal with dangerous or emergency situations quickly, but can be harmful if they occur too often.

The parasympathetic nervous system, on the other hand, causes a lowering of heart and respiratory rates and an increase in blood flow to the skin, digestive, urinary and reproductive systems. Indian Head Massage can activate the parasympathetic nervous system and stimulate blood flow to the skin and hair follicles, improving the condition of both skin and hair.

The diagram shows the distribution of the cranial nerves. As you can see, there are many nerve endings on the face. The gentle touch applied during treatment sends relaxing messages to the brain.

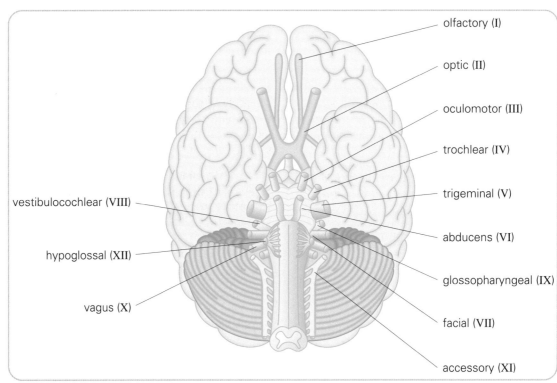

olfactory (I)

optic (II)

oculomotor (III)

trochlear (IV)

trigeminal (V)

abducens (VI)

glossopharyngeal (IX)

facial (VII)

accessory (XI)

vestibulocochlear (VIII)

hypoglossal (XII)

vagus (X)

The cranial nerves

The 12 cranial nerves (I-XII)
Olfactory nerve (I)
Sends information about smells from the inside of the nose to the brain's olfactory centres.

Optic nerve (II)
Sends visuals signals and connects the retina with the brain via a bundle of approximately a million fibres.

Oculomotor (III), trochlear (IV) and abducent nerves (VI)
Regulate voluntary movements of eye muscles and eyelids, dilate the pupil and shape the lense to focus on near objects.

Trigeminal nerve (V)
Relays sensory information from the eyes, face and teeth. It also has certain motor functions (biting, chewing and swallowing). Its three major branches are called ophthalmic, maxillary and mandibular nerve.

Facial nerve (VII)
Branches of this nerve connect to the taste buds, the skin of the outer ear, the salivary and lacrimal (tear) glands, and control the muscles used for facial expressions.

Vestibulocochlear (auditory) nerve (VIII)
Its branches send information about sound (cochlear nerve) as well as balance and the orientation of the head (vestibular nerve) to the brain.

Glossopharyngeal (IX) and hypoglossal (XII) nerves
Contain motor fibres for swallowing and sensory fibres that relay information on taste, touch and heat from the tongue and pharynx.

Vagus nerve (X)
A mixed nerve supplying motor fibres to the muscles of swallowing and parasympathetic fibres to the heart and other large organs of the chest cavity and abdomen. Sensory branches carry impulses from these organs and the sensation of taste from the mouth.

Accessory nerve (XI)
Innervates muscles in the shoulders and neck, the pharynx and larynx, and contributes to the production of voice.

The cranial nerves

FAQs

What makes hair curly or straight?

This depends on the shape of the follicles from which the hair grows. The follicle moulds the developing hair, which is pushed up through the follicle towards the surface of the skin by new cells forming underneath. As it pushes up, the cells harden (keratinise) to form hair. Some hair follicles are straight and cylindrical, which result in straight hair, while others are oval shaped or flattened, in which case the person will have wavy or kinky hair. Of course there are degrees in between, but the flatter the follicle the curlier the hair, and the rounder the follicle the straighter the hair.

Is it true that people living in very cold climates have little body or facial hair?

Yes, this is true. If there is little hair, moisture cannot be trapped near the skin's surface where it can freeze and cause frostbite. Similarly, tightly coiled hair, such as that seen on people of African origin, aids cooling by allowing sweat to evaporate, as the hair doesn't spread and stick to the skin.

What is hair analysis?

This is chemical analysis of a hair sample. It is widely used in forensics (e.g. crime identification) and toxicology (determining levels of toxic chemicals or drugs in the body). Some complementary and alternative therapists as well as medical practitioners analyse hair samples to check for nutritional deficiencies and imbalances. Hair samples are easy to take and can show what has passed from the bloodstream to the follicle in the previous 6–8 weeks.

other recommended therapies

An important aspect of the holistic approach to health is being able to recognise the limitations of the treatment you offer. A diligent professional therapist is aware of the benefits of other treatments and knows when to refer clients to a medical practitioner or to a more appropriate complementary or alternative therapy. Even though they are frequently grouped together, a distinction may be made between complementary and alternative medicine. Complementary therapies do not focus on diagnosing or curing disease, but can be used simultaneously with conventional medicine to reduce side effects and stress and to increase well-being. Alternative therapies such as osteopathy, chiropractic, acupuncture, herbal medicine and homeopathy, all have an individual diagnostic approach and can in some instances be used in place of conventional medicine. In this chapter we discuss some of the main complementary and alternative therapies. If you are a therapist, you should experience some of these therapies yourself so that you have first-hand knowledge to pass on to your clients, as well as benefiting your own well-being.

Acupressure

This is a traditional Chinese bodywork technique that is based on the same ideas as acupuncture but without the use of needles. It involves placing physical pressure (by hand, elbow or with various devices) on points on the surface of the body to release blocked energy and bring about relief through greater balance and circulation of energy in the body. Depth of pressure and length of time applied are important aspects of the treatment. This treatment can be performed through clothing.

Acupuncture

An ancient Chinese technique involving the insertion of fine needles just under the skin in specific locations, according to a mapping of energy pathways (meridians), to relieve pain and treat a wide variety of complaints. Acupuncture can be beneficial in a wide range of medical conditions, including neurological, gastrointestinal, mental and emotional. It is commonly used to control pain and to treat chronic conditions such as allergies or addictions. Disposable needles are used for hygiene and safety purposes.

Alexander technique

Frederick Mathias Alexander (1868–1955), an Australian actor, developed this technique after discovering that improving his posture stopped him losing his voice. It is usually taught in individual lessons, during which the student becomes aware of unconscious bad habits and patterns in their everyday activities, including walking, sitting, standing, bending and lifting. Alexander technique provides a means for overcoming these habits by teaching clients how to stop interfering with their body's innate co-ordination and guiding them through simple movements to become aware of proper physical function. Alexander technique is especially useful for treating backaches and headaches, which are often due to poor posture.

Aromatherapy

This is a system of caring for the body and mind with essential oils extracted from flowers and plants. These essential oils, which are highly concentrated, can be added to a bath, massaged through the skin, inhaled directly, used with teas, or vaporised in a room. Aromatherapy is intended to relieve pain, care for the skin and alleviate tension and fatigue.

Ayurveda

Ayurveda is an ancient system of preventive healthcare, practised in India for 5000 years. Ayurveda means 'knowledge of life' and according to this system, bodily health is determined by three biological principles, called doshas: vata, which regulates movement; pitta, which regulates metabolism; and kapha, which regulates structure. Ayurveda includes diet and herbal remedies and emphasises the use of body, mind, and spirit in disease prevention and treatment.

Bach flower remedies

This is a group of 38 energetic essences derived from various flowers by the British physician and homeopath Dr. Edward Bach in the early twentieth century. Based on the theory that physical ailments as well as psychological problems arise from emotional

Essential oils have many benefits

Bach Flower remedies can ease many emotional problems

states, particular herbs and flowers are used to treat mental and emotional problems such as fear, loneliness or despair. Practitioners prescribe essences that can affect the client's energy field, promoting equilibrium.

Bowen technique

This technique is named after Australian Tom Bowen, an industrial chemist, who in the 1950s introduced the concept of having periods of rest between a series of movements within a treatment session. It uses light rolling movements on muscle and connective tissue to release tension, balance the body and stimulate energy flow. It is a gentle process that encourages the body to heal itself. The technique was limited to Australia until Bowen's death in 1982, when it was named and spread by Bowen's apprentices.

Chiropractic

The World Federation of Chiropractic defines chiropractic as:

'A health profession concerned with the diagnosis, treatment and prevention of mechanical disorders of the musculo-skeletal system, and the effects of these disorders on the function of the nervous system and general health. There is an emphasis on manual treatments including spinal manipulation or adjustment.'

The practitioner manipulates the joints of the body, specifically the spine, in order to relieve pain. It works on the basis that pain is often caused by a nerve that is not functioning properly, so the spine, which houses the central nervous system, is the focus of the therapy. It is especially useful for lower back or neck pains as well as headaches.

Counselling

This is a therapy in which a trained person listens to a client's problems and anxieties and advises without judging, to help them find their own answers. It can help a person to resolve conscious conflicts and focus on setting goals and problem solving. A wide variety of techniques may be used, including verbal communication. Counsellors assist the client to focus on constructive behaviour, which will help them reach specific goals.

Herbal medicine (herbalism)

This holistic system is one of the oldest forms of medicine involving the use of plants to maintain health and treat illness. Particular emphasis is laid on the energetic content of the plant and its ability to stimulate healing. The whole herb is regarded as having a greater healing potential than a single active agent (as used by the pharmaceutical industry). Herbal medicine is given in many forms, including liquids, infusions, tablets, creams, poultices and ointments. Herbs are used in both Eastern and Western medicine.

Homeopathy

This is a system of natural medicine developed by Samuel Hahnemann, a highly respected German doctor, in the late eighteenth century. Homeopathy is based on the law of similars in that 'like cures like'. The word 'homeopathy' comes from Greek 'homoios', meaning similar, and 'pathos', meaning suffering. Homeopathic remedies are substances given in a diluted and potentised form to stimulate the body's own healing potential. Where a sick person is showing symptoms of a disease, a homeopathic remedy is capable of curing those symptoms, whereas in a healthy person it might produce them. Remedies have to be stored well away from strong-smelling substances, because such smells can reduce their effectiveness.

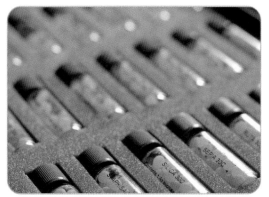
Homeopathic remedies stimulate the body's own healing potential

Iridology

This is a fascinating diagnostic system stating that every bodily organ corresponds to a location on the iris, the coloured portion of the eye surrounding the pupil. The markings and changes on the iris are studied for indications of any irregularities that may indicate health problems.

Kinesiology

This technique was originally developed by a chiropractor in the 1960s and has since been incorporated into the practice of many disciplines, including health, education and psychology. Kinesiology tests muscle strength to identify substances that can disturb or support the client's well-being. For example, it can be used to find which foods are most conducive to health and those that may cause unwanted symptoms, or to find the most appropriate natural medicine, such as a nutritional supplement, homeopathic remedy or essential oil.

Osteopathy

Osteopathy is a system of healthcare founded by an American doctor, Andrew Taylor Still (1828–1917). Osteopathy means 'bone disease', indicating the relationship between disorder and the misalignment of bones. By manipulating joints and bones, osteopaths can correct structural problems, which improves the body's function. Osteopathy treats structure and function as interdependent, so if the structure is damaged in any way, it follows that it will affect the function. For example, a distortion of the pelvic bones could alter the position of the uterus, and possibly result in miscarriage. An injury or weakness in the lower part of the spine often results in misalignment of the vertebrae, leading to tight shoulder or neck muscles and restricted movement. Massage offers temporary relief but osteopathic treatment can adjust the misalignment and provide more permanent relief.

casestudy

This story from Sue, an Indian Head Massage therapist, demonstrates when it may be appropriate to recommend other therapies to clients:

'Deidre's main problems were frequent severe headaches and stiff shoulders. Her company provided on-site massage so she had regular sessions. When she arrived for treatments I noticed that her shoulders were raised and were usually very painful to touch. I spent extra time on her shoulders and sometimes used a massage tool. I would start lightly and gradually increase pressure as the muscles softened. If she arrived with a headache, this would usually be gone before I had touched her head and she said I had 'magic fingers'! By the end of a treatment her shoulders would be relaxed and lowered and her headaches gone. However, one week later the stiff shoulders and headache would return. I thought the severely stiff shoulders could be due to be a lower back problem that was pushing her spine out of alignment and possibly causing headaches. Deidre recalled an old injury suffered years earlier while doing gymnastics and on my recommendation, she saw an osteopath. The osteopath confirmed that the old injury was causing her shoulder problem and after several osteopathic treatments her shoulders and headaches were greatly alleviated. She continued to have regular Indian Head Massage and was delighted to finally resolve her shoulder and headache problems.'

Physiotherapy

Physiotherapy (also known as physical therapy) is a health profession concerned with the assessment, diagnosis, and treatment of disease and disability through physical means. It is based upon principles of medical science, and is held to be within the sphere of conventional rather than alternative medicine. Physiotherapy uses physical exercises, massage and the application of pressure to relieve pain and muscular tension. It is often used to re-educate the body in cases of major surgery, illness or accident.

Reflexology

Reflexology is based on the principle that there are reflex points on the feet and hands that correspond and connect to all parts of the body. The use of pressure to stimulate these points can release stress and tension, stimulate circulation, restore balance throughout the body and induce a state of deep relaxation.

Reiki

Reiki is a system of healing developed in the early 1900s by Mikao Usui in Japan. It is a healing art passed from Master to student. The word comes from two Japanese words – 'rei' and 'ki', meaning Universal Life Force Energy. The term 'reiki' is used to describe both the energy and the Usui system of using it. The original system by Usui was called Usui Reiki Ryoho. There are many variants of reiki being practised nowadays. Reiki uses hands in certain positions on or above different parts of the body and the healer is said to draw energy to the body, promoting healing, balance and relaxation.

Shiatsu

Literally meaning 'finger pressure' this is a massage technique developed in Japan and based on the principle that disease and pain are caused by blocked energy along meridians in the body. By applying finger or thumb pressure to the blocked meridian, relief from pain and disease may result. Shiatsu is usually carried out with the client fully clothed.

Swedish body massage

Swedish body massage is based on techniques developed in the eighteenth and nineteenth centuries by Per Henrik Ling and Johan Georg Mezger (see also Chapter 1). The technique involves a sequence of movements that work superficially and deeper into the tissue layers, though it is generally considered a deep massage system. Movements such as stroking (effleurage) work over the skin to produce relaxation, whereas petrissage is a deeper technique that includes movements such as wringing and kneading to relieve tension in muscles. Treatments such as back massage or stress massage are adaptations of Swedish massage, whereas treatments such as aroma-therapy are usually lighter and concentrate on lymph drainage. Holistic massage uses Swedish massage techniques adapted to the needs of our modern and often stressful life. By treating the whole person it aims to relax muscles, calm emotions, improve circulation, recharge the body's immune system, refresh the spirit and balance the life-force.

Yoga and meditation

Both these self-help therapies have well-documented beneficial effects on mind and body. Yoga uses physical exercise, including postures, relaxation techniques and breathing exercises. Meditation uses a focus such as visualisation, a candle or a mantra to help a person find inner calm. This can allow the body to go into the healing and recharging mode it adopts when we sleep, allowing muscles to relax and body systems to become more efficient.

Yoga and meditation benefit both mind and body

FAQs

Do you know of any other treatments for alopecia areata as I suffer from this condition and find it quite depressing and worrying?

A study published in the August 2006 issue of the *Journal of the American Academy of Dermatology* reported good news for people with alopecia areata. Researchers used hypnotherapy to treat twenty-one alopecia patients who had lost at least 30 per cent of their scalp hair and had not been helped by steroids, a conventional approach to this disorder. Most patients were also receiving other medical treatments for the condition during the study. Every three weeks, the patients had a hypnosis session, during which the therapist made a number of suggestions, including imagining the healing effects of the sun on their scalps. After three or four sessions, hair growth on at least 75 per cent of the scalp occurred among twelve of the twenty-one patients, with nine experiencing total hair re-growth. During the follow-up period, five of the patients had relapses. The researchers are not sure if hypnosis was responsible for the improvements they saw or how hypnosis might stimulate hair growth. However, they speculated it might lead to changes in the immune system. As well as regular head massage with oils and management of your stress levels, you could also try some visualisation exercises. It is advisable to see a qualified nutritionist as your diet may need improvement or supplementation.

If I recommend other types of treatments to my clients, am I likely to lose them as clients?

No, clients generally continue to have Indian Head Massage after referral for other treatments, and they are extremely grateful that you have pointed them in the right direction to suit their needs.

where to go from here

Now that you have finished reading 'Indian Head Massage in Essence' you may decide you want to learn more and perhaps undertake a training course. If so, your options are:

- to find an introductory course that will enable you to carry out a treatment on family and friends
- to get a professional qualification in Indian Head Massage.

Introductory courses

Most further and adult education colleges and some private colleges offer introductory courses in Indian Head Massage. These will not give you a professional qualification but you will learn some practical techniques and find out if it is something you would like to study in more depth.

Courses leading to a professional qualification

Professional Indian Head Massage courses are widely available in most further and adult education colleges and some private colleges.

The following points may help you decide which is best for you:

- Most professional courses require that you have a Level 3 qualification in anatomy and physiology. If you are already a qualified complementary therapist, it is likely that you already have this qualification. Your local college should be able to provide advice and guidance on the entry requirements for attending their professional Indian Head Massage courses.

- Some private colleges offer professional Indian Head Massage courses that do not have any entry requirements. You should check with them beforehand to ensure that the syllabus contains essential anatomy and physiology and that the qualification will allow you to practise professionally and get insurance. They should also be able to give you a list of reputable insurers who will cover you to practise professionally.

Whatever course you decide on, Indian Head Massage is a good starting point for anyone interested in a career in massage.

casestudy

Gavin, a musician, talks about the Indian Head Massage taster day that changed his life! He has now completed a professional training course in Indian Champissage, is studying for his anatomy and physiology diploma and has signed up for another massage course.

'I originally joined the one-day taster class in Champissage, hoping I would learn some techniques to alleviate the tension headaches and migraines my wife Ewa suffers from. Little did I realise just how beneficial I would find the taster day, both for my wife and as a source of inspiration for myself. The techniques I learnt, I put into practice on my wife with immediate positive effects: the ache in her back, stiff neck and tension headaches were all targeted and their severity decreased. Over the next few weeks, as I continued to treat my wife, I realised I had found a skill which brought both relief and relaxation to others, a skill I was happy and eager to develop. Having only limited experience of professional massage, the training process, the course and the case studies have proved extremely interesting, both in terms of reactions to the treatments given and what I have learned from the experience. In many ways, I find a certain similarity with my music; learning physical techniques which are refined through practice and experience and through building a relationship with the recipient.'

CPD for qualified therapists

If you are a qualified complementary therapist looking to top up your skills, you are probably also a member of a professional organisation and aware that most organisations require their members to undertake a minimum number of continuing professional development (CPD) hours annually. Even without this requirement, it is very important to keep up to date on trends in the industry and to update your skills. CPD maintains high professional standards through increased knowledge and awareness. It is also good marketing for your practice and will add to your client base!

Indian Head Massage is an ideal treatment to add to your repertoire. As well as offering it in your current practice, it is excellent for dealing with stress in the workplace. The Government's Health and Safety Executive (HSE) defines stress as: 'the adverse reaction that people have to excessive pressure or other types of demand placed on them' and their research has confirmed that:

- work-related stress accounts for over a third of all new incidences of ill health
- each case of stress-related ill health leads to an average of 30.9 working days lost

a total of 12.8 million working days were lost to stress, depression and anxiety in 2004/5.

(www.hse.gov.uk/stress)

Under the Management of Health and Safety at Work Regulations 1999, employers have duties to assess the risk of stress-related ill health arising from work activities, and under the Health and Safety at Work Act 1974 they are obliged to take measures to control that risk. Many businesses now use on-site complementary therapies as a way of tackling workplace stress. This can reduce the amount of time taken off work, have a positive effect on employee commitment to work, staff performance, productivity, recruitment, retention and customer satisfaction and is good for organisational image and reputation. Due to its mobile nature, Indian Head Massage is one of the most popular workplace treatments.

Tips for Indian Head Massage in the workplace

- Prepare professional literature, such as brochures and business cards.
- For leads to corporate work, use your contacts in office environments or research companies in your area, preferably with staff numbering 50 or more. The decision-maker for staff benefits is usually the Human Resources (HR) Manager, so write to them, briefly describing the benefits of Indian Head Massage and follow up with a phone call. To help win business, offer a free treatment to the HR Manager.
- Do an internet search for on-site massage companies who may be able to offer you work.
- Decide how much you will charge and how long the treatments will be (15, 20 or 30 minutes). Companies will either meet the full cost or subsidise treatments; sometimes staff themselves meet the full cost, though in our experience this is not common.
- Work out how many treatments you can realistically do without becoming exhausted and make sure to build some breaks into your timetable. We recommend that the maximum number of massage hours in one day should be no more than five.
- Decide on the minimum number of massages you are prepared to do as it may not be worth your while financially unless you have at least five or six clients.
- Have a point of contact in the office who can arrange everything you need – an appropriate room to work in, a suitable chair – and make the bookings for you.
- Look neat and presentable, and behave in a professional manner at all times.
- Have a consultation form or checklist that is quick and easy to complete.

117

FAQs

I have heard about correspondence courses in Indian Head Massage. Is this a good way to learn?

A course in Indian Head Massage is a great way to meet other people who share a common interest and you will have the added bonus of receiving a regular head massage as students practise the techniques on each other. You will also have the support and guidance of your tutor, who will ensure that you are practising the treatment safely and effectively and will provide feedback on your progress. You will miss out on these important aspects if you undertake a correspondence course.

If a correspondence course is the only way for you, it is best to do one that involves some practical sessions with a tutor. Check with the provider that the course will be insurable and ask them for details of insurance companies who will cover you to practise. Do not make any commitment until you are satisfied with all the elements of any course you decide on and if possible speak to someone who has already done the course that you are interested in.

Do all Indian Head Massage courses involve case studies and examinations?

Case studies, where the student completes consultations and practises the treatment on 'clients' before they qualify, are an important part of any reputable Indian Head Massage course. They provide an opportunity to perfect the techniques and carry out the treatment without referring to your notes before you begin to practise professionally. Written and practical tests are also important to ensure that you have a good understanding of the underpinning theory and can carry out the treatment in a satisfactory and professional manner.

The professional Indian Head Massage course in my local college is a Level 3 course. Since I have no previous experience of Indian Head Massage will I have to do a Level 1 course first and progress to Level 3?

Depending on your previous educational experience you may be able to start with a Level 3 course. An entry level (or Level 1) course is an introductory course and will be sufficient if you want to find out about Indian Head Massage and learn some techniques to use on family and friends. For these courses you may obtain a certificate of attendance. Professional courses in Indian Head Massage are usually at Level 3, which is equivalent to A level standard. For a Level 3 course in Indian Head Massage (e.g. ITEC or VTCT), at least five GCSEs at grades A* to C (or equivalent) are recommended. However, this is at the discretion of the college and your previous educational and work experience will be taken into account. You will need to have a Level 3 qualification in anatomy and physiology and should be sufficiently fluent in English to follow lectures, participate in class discussions and answer questions in the theory exam paper. As this treatment requires the therapist to stand, you should be able to stand comfortably for the duration of a treatment (about 35 minutes).

Can Indian Head Massage be combined with another therapy?

Although Indian Head Massage is a complete therapy in its own right, some practitioners combine it with another therapy such as body massage or reiki, or use some of the Indian Head Massage movements, particularly on the shoulders, to relax a client before a reflexology session. See Chapter 9 for a list of other therapies.

Useful contacts
Indian Head Massage training courses

Approved training centres for Level 3 courses

ITEC (International Therapies Examination Council)
2nd floor, Chiswick Gate
598–608 Chiswick High Road
London W4 5RT
Tel: +44 (0)20 8994 4141
Fax: +44 (0)20 8994 7880
Web: www.itecworld.co.uk
Email: info@itecworld.co.uk

Vocational Training Charitable Trust (VTCT)
See http://www.vtct.org.uk for a list of training centres.

Private schools for accredited Indian Head Massage courses

London Centre of Indian Champissage International (LCICI)
Principal: Narendra Mehta
136 Holloway Road
London N7 8DD
Tel: +44 (0)20 7609 3590
www.indianchampissage.com

Hands on Training
Orchard Cottage
Maidstone Road
Matfield
Kent TN12 7LG
Tel: +44 (0)1892 725716
www.hands-on-training.net

Lesley Hart teaches CMA and CThA recognised courses in Indian Head Massage, Ear Candling and Natural Facial, and CMA recognised courses in Facial Radiance.
Tel: +44 (0)20 84621886
Email: lesley@hands-on-training.net
www.hands-on-training.net

Mary Dalgleish teaches CMA recognised courses in Indian Head Massage for LCICI. She also teaches ITEC courses and CThA approved CPD courses in Ear Candling, Natural Facials and Natural Face Lift Massage (Facial Rejuvenation).
Tel: +44 (0)20 8874 9047
Email: marydalgleish@yahoo.co.uk
www.head2toemassage.co.uk

Correspondence courses

The Kevala Centre
Hunsdon Road
Torquay
Devon TQ1 1QB
Phone: +44 (0)1803 215678
www.kevala.co.uk

Advanced Indian Head Massage courses

One-day CPD courses for therapists, covering topics including Ayurveda, marma points, use of oils and stress-busting massage techniques.
www.hands-on-training.net
www.head2toemassage.co.uk

Find an Indian Head Massage therapist

www.indianchampissage.com
www.hands-on-training.net
www.the-cma.org.uk
www.embodyforyou.co.uk
www.fht.org.uk
www.iptiuk.com
www.healthypages.net
www.complementarytherapists.org

119

Insurance for Indian Head Massage

www.towergategroup.co.uk
www.iptiuk.com
www.balen.co.uk
www.babtac.com

Ireland:
ARCHTI www.complementarytherapists.org
Tel: +353 053–9383734
Email: info@complementarytherapists.org
www.irishtherapists.ie

Massage for babies and children

www.iaim.org.uk
www.massageinschools.com
www.massageinschoolsassociation.com

Naturopathy advice for therapists

Janna Land
Tel: 07973 107126
Email: info@jannaland.co.uk
www.jannaland.co.uk

Useful products

Chakra meditation CD

This beautiful two-track CD entitled 'A Journey Through the Chakras' explains subtle energy, the various layers of the aura and the chakras, before taking you through a meditation on the seven major chakras from the base to the crown.
To purchase, contact:
Mary Dalgleish
Tel: +44 (0)20 8874 9047
Web: www.head2toemassage.co.uk
Email: marydalgleish@yahoo.co.uk

Ayurvedic hair oil

Hands on Training
Tel: +44 (0)20 8462 1886
Email: lesley@hands-on-training.net
www.hands-on-training.net

Massage oils

The Neem People
The Barn, Denant Mill
Dreenhill, Haverfordwest
Pembrokeshire SA62 3TS
Tel/Fax: +44 (0)1437 764415
Email: mailto:sidvin@btinternet.com
www.theneempeople.com

Essentially Oils
8–10 Mount Farm, Junction Road
Churchill, Chipping Norton
Oxfordshire OX7 6NP
Tel: +44 (0)1608 659544 (6 lines)
Email: sales@essentiallyoils.com
www.essentiallyoils.com

G. Baldwin & Co
171/173 Walworth Road
London SE17 1RW
Tel: +44 (0)20 7703 5550
Email: sales@baldwins.co.uk
www.baldwins.co.uk

Therapy cushions

Darley Couches (ask for aromatherapy cushion which is ideal for head massage)
Tel: +44 (0)1208 873 200
Email: stephatdarley@aol.com
www.darleycouches.co.uk

Massage tools

www.omnimassage.com
www.omnimassage.co.uk

Low-cost and free business cards

www.vistaprint.co.uk

Nutritional supplements

Revital Ltd
78 High Street
Ruislip
Middx HA4 7AA
Tel: 0207 076 6615
Mail order hotline: 0800 252 875
www.revital.com

Higher Nature
Burwash Common
East Sussex TN19 7LX
Tel: +44 (0)1435 884668
Email: info@higher-nature.co.uk
www.highernature.co.uk

Viridian Nutrition
31 Alvis Way
Daventry
Northamptonshire NN11 5PG
Tel: +44 (0)1327 878335
Email: info@viridian-nutrition.com
www.viridian-nutrition.com

Bibliography and further reading

Ashley-Farrand, Thomas (1999) *Healing Mantras*, Gateway Publications

Brunton, Paul (2004) *A Search in Secret India*, Cosmo Publications, India

Buck, Phillipa and Bensouilah, Janetta (2005) 'Nut allergies in children – are massage oils safe?' *CAM* magazine (January 2005)

Davis, Patricia (1991) *Subtle Aromatherapy*, CW Daniels, UK

Earle, Liz (2002) *New Vital Oils*, Vermilion, London

Frawley, Dr David, Ranade, Dr Subbash and Lele, Dr Avinash (2003) *Ayurveda and Marma Therapy*, Lotus Press, USA

Harding, Jennie (2006) *Stress Management in Essence*, Hodder Arnold, London

Iyengar, B K S (1988) *Light on Yoga*, Harper Collins

Jenkins, Nicola (2006) *Massage in Essence*, Hodder Arnold, London

Johari, Harish (1996) *Ayurvedic Massage*, Healing Arts Press, Rochester, Vermont

Leadbeater, C W (1994) *The Chakras*, Quest Books, The Theosophical Publishing House, USA

McGuinness, Helen (2004) *Indian Head Massage*, Hodder and Stoughton

Marsden, Kathryn (2002) *Superskin*, Thorsons, London

Mehta, Narendra (1999) *Indian Head Massage*, Thorsons, London

Omraam Mikhael Aivanhov (1986) *Man's Subtle Bodies and Centres*, Editions Prosveta, France

Ozaniec, Naomi (1991) *The Elements of The Chakras*, Element Books, UK

Page, Dr Christine R (1992) *Frontiers of Health*, C W Daniels, UK

Sachs, Melanie (2005) *Ayurvedic Beauty Care*, Motilal Banarsidass Publishers, Delhi

Sharamon, Shalila and Baginski, Bodo J (1991) *The Chakra Handbook*, Lotus Light Publications, USA

Time Life Education (1988) *India, Library of Nations*

Websites

http://en.wikipedia.org
www.news/bbc.co.uk/1/health/4793634.stm (migraine and hole in the heart)
www.healer.ch
http://auraphoto.com
www.ayurvedainstitute.org
http//www.massagemag.com/2002/issue100/history100.htm
www.youthingstrategies.com
www.coconut-connections.com
www.coconutresearchcenter.org

glossary

Acne: An inflammatory disorder of sebaceous glands of the face, back and chest, characterised by blackheads, pimples and in severe cases, cysts and scars. It is most common during puberty due to overactivity of sebaceous glands, stimulated by sex hormones.

Adhesions: Abnormal bands of tissue that grow in the body at the joints, e.g. between shoulder joint surfaces in cases of frozen shoulder (*adhesive capulitis*).

Amenorrhea: Abnormal suppression or absence of menstruation.

Androgen: Substance producing or stimulating male characteristics, such as the male hormone testosterone.

Antimicrobial: A substance that inhibits growth of micro-organisms including bacteria, viruses and fungi.

Atopic: A person is atopic if they have an inherited tendency for developing allergies.

Avicenna: Avicenna (980–1037) was a Persian physician, philosopher, and scientist. He was the author of 450 books on a wide range of subjects. Many of these concentrated on philosophy and medicine and he is considered by many to be 'the father of modern medicine'.

Bacteria: Bacteria are unicellular living organisms living on or within larger living organisms, including humans. Some produce disease and are called 'pathogenic', but some are useful (e.g. bacteria that produce nitrogen in soil or 'friendly bacteria' in the digestive system). Pathogenic bacteria cause disease by gaining access to tissues and multiplying to damage their surroundings or by releasing toxins that poison remote parts of the body. Antibiotics are commonly used to kill or inhibit bacteria but they must not be used indiscriminately, because continued exposure to a particular antibiotic results in the development of resistant strains of bacteria. Some bacterial skin conditions such as impetigo are contraindicated to massage.

Borage (Starflower): An annual herb with rough hairy stems and leaves, used in cooking since the middle ages. Folk remedies claimed it could instil courage and dispel sadness. It has blue star-shaped flowers, the seeds of which are used to produce oil containing gamma-linolenic acid (GLA), an Omega-6 oil that supports healthy skin and hair and reduces joint inflammation, swelling and pain.

Buddhism: A religion based on the teachings of Siddhartha Gautama, known as Buddha. There are several Buddhist sects, all teaching paths to Nirvana (enlightenment or bliss). Buddha refuted the idea of man's having an immortal soul and did not preach of any Supreme Deity. Instead he taught that man should seek freedom from desire, greed, hatred and delusion, and seek enlightenment through recognising existence and the source of suffering and following a path of correct understanding, behaviour and meditation. Although Buddha was idolised, he never claimed to be anything more than a man.

Caste system: Originally the system of the four hereditary classes into which Indian population was divided: 1) descendants of Brahma – seers (priests, teachers); 2) warriors – military leaders, business owners; 3) mercantile – skilled craftspersons; and 4) the lowest or agricultural class – servants or unskilled labourers. From these four, hundreds of divisions and minor castes have sprung.

Chlorella: A type of algae (seaweed) that is high in protein and other essential nutrients. When dried, it is about 45 per cent protein, 20 per cent fat, 20 per cent carbohydrate, and 10 per cent various minerals and vitamin.

Cirrhosis: Inflammation and subsequent hardening of an organ, particularly the liver. Cirrhosis of the liver is a chronic condition, often associated with alcohol or drug abuse but it can also be caused by diseases such as hepatitis.

Cold-pressing: This term describes the extraction of oil from a plant or part of a plant by using pressure to squeeze out the oil, without the use of heat. The use of heat can change the chemistry of the oil, making it less pure.

Congenital: A condition believed to have been present since birth, including inherited conditions or those caused by environmental factors. Congenital skin conditions include eczema and psoriasis, which are not contraindicated to Indian Head Massage but the area should be avoided if inflamed or sore.

Cross-infection: Infection transmitted between individuals infected with different pathogenic (disease carrying) micro-organisms.

Desquamation: The shedding or peeling of the outer layer (*stratum corneum*) of the skin.

Dopamine: A neurotransmitter, or chemical that transmits signals between nerve cells, found in regions of the brain that regulate movement, emotion, motivation and feelings of pleasure. Reduced levels of dopamine are found in those with Parkinson's disease.

Dyslexia: Disorder involving difficulties in reading, which may include word-blindness and a tendency to reverse letters and words in reading and writing.

Eczema/dermatitis: The terms 'eczema' and 'dermatitis' are used synonymously. The word 'eczema' comes from Greek and means 'to boil over'. A person with severe eczema can appear as if their skin is burnt. It can be found all over the body but appears most often on the inside of the knee and elbow joints and on the face, hands and scalp. The skin becomes dry and itchy, causing great discomfort, but the condition is not contagious. The underlying cause is usually an allergy to many things, including foods, fabrics and skin lotions. The disorder may begin in month-old babies and usually subsides by age three, but may flare again between the ages of ten and twelve and last through puberty or beyond. Eczema or dermatitis due to allergies is termed 'atopic'.

Ether: Also called 'akash' or 'quintessence', an invisible essence that pervades all form and all other elements. It is the fifth and highest element after air, earth, fire and water and is believed to be the substance composing all heavenly bodies. It is the subtlest of the five elements that make up the physical universe.

Fungal infection: A type of infection caused by yeasts and moulds. Fungal skin infections include ringworm and athlete's foot, both of which are contagious. Fungal infections usually itch.

Head lice: Head lice (*Pediculosis capitis*) is an infestation affecting the scalp, though sometimes the eyebrows, eyelashes and beard. Infestation is particularly common in children, especially girls. The lice feed on blood from the scalp and are transmitted by direct contact of hair and items such as combs, towels and headgear. The bites cause severe itching and the lesions may become infected. The glands of the neck may sometimes enlarge. Adult lice may be seen around the back of the head and behind the ears. The small eggs (nits) are easier to detect, as they are firmly attached to hair shafts. These hatch in 3 to 14 days and may be removed by a nit comb. The scalp should be treated and members of the same household examined for infestation. Some essential oils such as tea tree and eucalyptus are effective in treating head lice.

Hinduism: The world's oldest organised religion, based on ancient Vedic literature and in existence for 4500 years. Hindus have many different practices varying from country to country, even from community to community. Reincarnation, a caste system and being held accountable for one's deeds (karma), are fundamental components of Hinduism. Ancient gods (especially Brahma, Vishnu, and Shiva) are commonly interpreted as representations of the various aspects of the divine (Brahman).

Impetigo: A highly contagious skin infection caused by bacteria, usually occurring around the nose and mouth; commonly in children. The symptoms are inflammation with isolated pustules, which become crusty and rupture.

Jainism: Jainism, traditionally known as 'Jain Dharma', is a religion and philosophy originating in ancient India. Although now a minority in modern India there are growing communities in the United States, Western Europe, Africa and the Far East. Jains have continued to sustain the ancient ascetic tradition of abstaining from worldly pleasures. Jainism stresses spiritual independence and equality of all life with a particular emphasis on non-violence and self-control.

Kyphosis: An abnormally increased curvature of the thoracic spine, resulting in a round-shouldered appearance.

Lordosis: An exaggeration of the curve of the lumbar spine, giving the appearance of a hunched back.

Male-pattern baldness: Also known as androgenetic alopecia, this is hair loss that is genetically determined and hormone dependent. It is common in males, although women can carry the genetic disposition. It begins with frontal recession and progresses to leave a sparse rim of hair.

Mantra: Mantra is a Sanskrit word meaning 'divine speech'. This use of mantras is designed to generate sound waves to promote healing and higher awareness. The practice originated in Hinduism and Buddhism, and mantras are usually Sanskrit words, such as 'OM'. Speaking or even thinking of a mantra can positively influence the chakras and physical body.

Monounsaturated: Refers to the chemistry of fats or oils that have one double bond. Double bonds give fatty acids their benefits. Monounsaturated fats are found in plant oils such as olive or avocado and can provide health benefits without clogging up the arteries.

Naturopathy: A holistic medical system that treats health conditions by using the body's innate ability to heal. It is a drugless system of

therapy, making use of physical forces such as air, light, water, heat and massage rather than surgery or medicine to treat disease.

New Age: A term used to describe a broad movement that emerged in the late twentieth century in Western cultures, characterised by an individual approach to spiritual exploration that is not aligned to a specific religion.

Organic oils: Oils derived from wild or untreated sources where no pesticides or chemical fertilisers have been applied.

Osteophyte: A small abnormal bony outgrowth, also called 'a bone spur', occurring at sites of cartilage degeneration or destruction near joints and intervertebral discs.

Oxidise: When a substance combines with oxygen, causing a chemical change and deterioration of that substance.

Patch test: The process of applying a product to a small part of the skin, usually in a non-visible area such as behind the ear, the inner arm or the back of the neck. This allows a person to find out if they are sensitive to the product without experiencing the discomfort of a major skin breakout if applied to large areas of skin.

Polycystic Ovarian Syndrome: Also known as 'Stein-Leventhal syndrome', this is a hormonal disorder characterised by incomplete development of maturing follicles in the ovary due to inadequate secretion of luteinising hormone, which triggers ovulation. The follicles fail to release ova and remain as multiple cysts, enlarging the ovary. Symptoms include acne, obesity, excessive hair growth (hirsutism) and irregular or no menstrual periods.

Polyunsaturated: Refers to the chemistry of fats or oils that have more than one double bond. These fats, which are vital for the health of the brain, nervous system, cardiovascular system and skin, are regarded as the healthiest of all fats. They fall into two types: Omega 3 (linolenic acid) found in oily fish, pumpkin and flax seeds; and Omega 6 (linoleic acid) found in sesame and sunflower seeds.

Psoriasis: A non-contagious disorder resulting from increased turnover of epidermal cells. The normal period from new cell to desquamation is 28 days, but for psoriasis sufferers this is reduced to 4 days. The condition is characterised by silvery scaly patches usually on the scalp, elbows, knees and genital region. Itching and nail changes are common (e.g. pitting and yellow discoloration resembling fungal infection). Psoriasis may also cause hair loss and arthritis (psoriatic arthritis). The cause is not fully understood, although it is considered to be an auto-immune disease where the body reacts against one of its own tissues or cell types.

Ringworm: Ringworm, also known as '*Tinea*', is a contagious fungal infection of the skin. It is common, especially among children, and may be spread by skin-to-skin contact, as well as contact with contaminated items such as hairbrushes. Ringworm spreads readily, as those infected are contagious even before they show symptoms of the disease. It appears as raised red swellings or lines that resemble burrowing worms – hence the name 'ringworm' – and includes diseases known as 'athlete's foot', 'jock itch', and 'ringworm of the scalp'. Humans can contract ringworm from animals: cats and dogs are often carriers.

Sanskrit: A classisical language that is one of 22 official languages of India. It has a status similar to that of Latin and forms a part of Hindu tradition.

Scabies: A highly contagious skin disorder caused by a mite that burrows into the skin and produces an intense, itchy rash. Since it is only 1/60th inch long, the scabies mite is almost impossible to see without magnification. The rash usually involves the hands, wrists, breasts, genital area, and waistline. In severe cases scabies can spread to almost the entire body, but rarely the face.

Scoliosis: An abnormal lateral curvature of the spine that can be mild to severe and affect people of all ages.

Serotonin: A hormone found in the brain, platelets, digestive tract, and pineal gland. It acts both as a neurotransmitter (a substance that nerves use to send messages to one another) and a vasoconstrictor (a substance that causes blood vessels to narrow). A lack of serotonin is thought to be a cause of depression and other disorders.

Shingles: Also called 'herpes zoster', this contagious disorder is due to infection of the ganglia of the posterior roots of the spinal nerves or the fifth cranial nerve by the varcella-zoster virus, which also causes chicken pox. It is marked by a painful eruption of small blisters, usually on one side of the body along the course of one or more nerves that affect the skin.

Sikhism: A religion based mostly in the Punjab province of India, blending aspects of Hinduism and Islam. Founded in the fifteenth century by Guru Nanak, Sikhism believes in one God and rejects idol worship and caste. Guru Nanak started free community kitchens where his followers could eat together, regardless of their caste.

Solvent extraction: A process of extracting essential oil from a raw material by exposing it to chemicals that strip away the non-soluble matter and leave the essential oil behind. This method is used for vegetable matter that is not very rich in aroma (bark, gums, resins) and animal matter (musk).

Spirulina: A type of blue-green algae (seaweed) that is rich in proteins and antioxidants.

Thyroxin: A hormone secreted by the thyroid gland that regulates metabolism, growth, development and the activity of the nervous system.

Ultraviolet (UV) light: Ninety-five per cent of the ultraviolet light from the sun is composed of UVA rays that cannot be felt as they do not burn skin. UVA is present in ordinary sunlight and can pass through clouds and glass. It causes ageing of the skin, damaging cells that produce collagen and elastin, reducing the skin's elasticity and firmness and encouraging wrinkles, pigmentation marks, lip thinning and allergies. UVB rays warm and tan the skin and overexposure causes sunburn. They also contribute to cell damage but do not pass through glass or cloudy skies. Both UVA and UVB rays alter DNA, the material inside the nucleus of cells that carries genetic information, and increase the risk of skin cancer.

Vasodilation: An increase in the size of a blood vessel caused by relaxation of the smooth muscle in the wall of the vessel.

Virus: A virus is the smallest type of microbe. It reproduces by invading a cell and taking over the cell's reproductive machinery, which it uses to produce hundreds of new viruses, often in less than an hour. The invaded cell (which is killed in the process) bursts and releases the viruses, which go on to invade other cells. Viruses can attack almost all living things – plants, animals and even bacteria. Most viruses are resistant to antibiotics. Viral skin infections include cold sores, shingles and warts.

index

Abbreviations used: IHM, Indian head massage.

131